Bad Times

Dr Noel Whiteside is a senior lecturer in the Department of Social Policy and Planning at the University of Bristol. Her historical research has concentrated on the nature of employment, its distribution, and the evolution of policies designed to alleviate labour market problems.

Noel Whiteside is the author of numerous articles in publications such as *Economic History Review, Historical Journal* and *Journal of Social Policy*, and has contributed chapters to several books. She is co-author of *Casual Labour* (Oxford University Press, 1985).

in the same series

Wealth and Inequality in Britain
W. D. Rubinstein

The Government of Space
Alison Ravetz

Educational Opportunities and Social Change in England
Michael Sanderson

A Property-owning Democracy?
M. J. Daunton

Sport in Britain
Tony Mason

The Labour Movement in Britain
John Saville

The Voluntary Impulse
Frank Prochaska

British Welfare Policy
Anne Digby

No Alternative? Unemployment in Britain
Sean Glynn

Judicial Punishment in England
J. A. Sharpe

A Tolerant Country?
Colin Holmes

BAD TIMES

Unemployment in British Social
and Political History

Noel Whiteside

faber and faber

LONDON · BOSTON

First published in 1991
by Faber and Faber Limited
3 Queen Square London WCIN 3AU

Photoset by Wilmaset Birkenhead Wirral
Printed in England by
Clays Ltd St Ives Plc
All rights reserved

A CIP record for this book is available from the British Library

ISBN 0–571–151574

For Stuart

HISTORICAL HANDBOOKS

Series Editors:
Avner Offer – University of York
F. M. L. Thompson – Institute of Historical Research,
University of London

It is widely recognized that many of the problems of present-day society are deeply rooted in the past, but the actual lines of historical development are often known only to a few specialists, while the policy-makers and analysts themselves frequently rely on a simplified, dramatized, and misleading version of history. Just as the urban landscape of today was largely built in a world that is no longer familiar, so the policy landscape is shaped by attitudes and institutions formed under very different conditions in the past. This series of specially commissioned handbooks aims to provide short, up-to-date studies in the evolution of current problems, not in the form of narratives but as critical accounts of the ways in which the present is formed by the past, and of the roots of present discontents. Designed for those with little time for extensive reading in the specialized literature, the books contain bibliographies for further study. The authors aim to be as accurate and comprehensive as possible, but not anodyne; their arguments, forcefully expressed, make the historical experience available in challenging form, but do not presume to offer ready-made solutions.

As it will be in the future, it was at the birth of man —
There are only four things certain since Social Progress began,
That the Dog returns to his Vomit and the Sow returns to her Mire
And the burnt Fool's bandaged finger goes wobbling back to the
Fire . . .

From Rudyard Kipling, 'The Gods of the Copybook Headings'

Contents

	Preface	xi
I	The Recent Crisis	1
II	Historical Perspectives	21
III	Theory and Opinion: The Politics of Unemployment	49
IV	Redefining Unemployment: The Interwar Years	69
V	State Training and Employment Policies	90
VI	Comparisons and Conclusions	110
	Notes	134
	Select Bibliography	136
	Index	141

Preface

'We must understand what is old to appreciate what is new.'
Mies van der Rohe

Until relatively recently, Britain's unemployment problem was viewed as a temporary aberration from an assumed 'norm' of full employment. The crisis was explained largely in economic terms. Rising oil prices and falling world trade, over-ambitious wage claims and the need to control inflation: all were referred to as fundamental causes for industrial stagnation and the consequent loss of jobs. By the mid-1980s, however, the economy was expanding, inflation had fallen, world trade was recovering, oil prices had slumped and the power of the trade unions had reached an all-time low. Yet unemployment hovered around the 3 million mark and there were fewer people in full-time work than at the beginning of the decade. Apparent economic recovery had not produced the expected solution.

In the absence of any other perspective on the question, unemployment has been relegated to the back burner of British politics, a source of political disquiet but no longer an issue to make or break governments. To many, it appears that nothing can be done.

Those with any recollection of the 1930s will be aware that we have been through all this before. This is not the first time that technological developments and changing patterns of world trade have threatened the job security of large numbers of workers. Nor is it the first time that central government has claimed that state intervention can do nothing to improve matters. Yet many analysts of the unemployment problem have dismissed historical precedent as irrelevant to the present situation and assert, often from a position of ignorance, that the study of the past is of antiquarian interest only, having no bearing on the nature of recent crises, nor on the measures taken for their amelioration. This book will challenge such assumptions. It will establish how far the nature of unemployment has changed since the industrial revolution, while demonstrating the continuities between past and present policies for the unemployed. It will demonstrate how an understanding of the problem depends less on the vagaries of economic demand than on the way the issue has been socially and politically constructed over a long period of time.

Unemployment as a social problem is best understood within an historical framework. The purpose of this book is to develop that framework, to provide those interested in the issue with a different perspective to the one commonly used by economic analysts. As such, it complements Sean Glynn's *No Alternative? Unemployment in Britain* (Faber and Faber, 1991), which explores economic aspects of the issue which are not dealt with here.

Dr Noel Whiteside
Dec. 1989

I

The Recent Crisis

Introduction

In the mid-1980s, the official count of unemployment in Britain was over 3 million – representing an increase of about 2 million in a single decade. Even for those of us with a limited political memory, this situation was – and still is – incomprehensible. In the late 1960s, the possibility of half a million unemployed was politically unthinkable. This particular benchmark was passed by the Heath government in 1970. As unemployment continued to rise, so did media speculation concerning the point at which the nation would find the situation intolerable. Unemployment passed 1 million in 1975, under a Labour government. In 1979, a general election took place with 1.3 million out of work: an election won by the Conservative Party under the slogan 'Labour is not working', with Tory campaign posters depicting poignant pictures of lengthening dole queues. In eighteen months, between 1980 and 1982, unemployment more than doubled, reaching 3 million in March 1983 and staying there until 1988, when the figures began a slow descent. They are apparently due to rise again in 1990. The notion that the British electorate would not tolerate high levels of unemployment has been shown to be quite fallacious. Twice in the 1980s, Margaret Thatcher has been returned to office, having presided over unemployment levels unprecedented in Britain's history.

The political climate has undergone a fundamental change. In the aftermath of the Second World War, all political parties had been committed to the principle of full employment. This meant that, in its management of the national economy, government aimed to secure jobs for all while promoting growth and prosperity. Folk memories of the degradation and waste associated with the high unemployment of the 1930s ensured that this priority remained at the top of the political agenda. Not only Britain, but all major industrial economies of the western world, remembered the Slump and its consequences; all took steps to prevent their recurrence. In the 1950s, new techniques of economic management encouraged both politicians and public to believe the problem had finally been cracked. Mass unemployment – like cholera and typhus – was a scourge of a bygone age whose disappearance was a tribute to the powers of central planning and the inevitable march of human progress.

This conclusion has proved to be unfounded. Moreover, attitudes have changed. Memories of the interwar years have faded. The generation that could recall the 'devil's decade' – as the 1930s had been called – has passed into retirement. The civil servants and politicians who were charged with the formulation and implementation of full employment policies have left the public arena. Their place has been taken by others less concerned with the unemployment question as a matter of political priority, who feel that the problem has none of the pressing urgency that it acquired in the interwar years. And, as unemployment is evidently tolerable after all, there are few political pressures to make them change their minds.

Few direct comparisons have been made between the 1930s and the 1980s – largely because the economy and the labour market are very different today, thanks to the expansion of white-collar work and public sector employment. However, an unwritten assumption still exists that matters were definitely worse then than they are now. At the very general level of official statistics, this appears to be true. Registered unemployment peaked at 2.828 million in 1932, representing 22 per cent of the workers insured under the state unemployment scheme.[1] Although the numbers of unemployed claimants peaked at 3.312 million in 1986,[2] this figure represents a substantially lower percentage of today's workforce. However, comparisons relying on government statistics alone are very misleading. First, interwar figures are drawn from a scheme which did not cover the whole working population. Adjusted to compensate for this deficiency, the numbers out of work rise to nearly 3.4

million, or 17 per cent of the workforce. A proportion of these 'unemployed', moreover, were part-time, casual and short-time workers who were 'topping up' reduced earnings with unemployment benefits; there were 600,000 of them in 1932. Currently, these people are excluded from the official unemployment count. We know that there were 900,000 men in part-time employment in 1988 (albeit that 400,000 have second jobs). The figure for women is appreciably higher; 20 per cent of women of working age are in part-time work, making a total of over 4 million. If, for the sake of compatibility, those deemed 'temporarily stopped' are removed from the 1932 statistics, the number falls to just over 2.8 million – a rate of just over 13 per cent, which is much closer to our more recent experience.

The case, however, does not rest there. Official unemployment statistics in the 1980s reduced the incidence of the problem in ways the adjusted figures for the 1930s did not. From 1982, official returns were based on successful claims for state benefits, not on numbers registering as out of work, which was the previously accepted system. In recent years, therefore, the government has been able to reduce 'unemployment' by reclassifying some claims for benefit and disqualifying others. We know that those unable to claim benefit before 1982 tended not to register as unemployed (the 'discouraged worker' syndrome); even so, this development has made it much harder to measure trends in unemployment over time, as each change in the regulations has a direct impact on the numbers deemed to be out of work. Between 1982 and 1986, around 400,000 unemployed were removed from official statistics through changes in administrative method. A high proportion of these are older workers; people taking 'early' retirement no longer 'count' as unemployed. Male economic activity rates for the 60–65-year-old age group slumped from 83 per cent in 1971 to 55 per cent in 1987 – but only a minority of the remaining 45 per cent 'count' as unemployed. Needless to say, such people would have been included in the interwar figures. Albeit that large numbers of long-term unemployed were – for all intents and purposes – in 'early retirement' in the Slump years, registration at the employment exchanges remained vital as official unemployment relief gave most the only income they could get.

Over and above this, there is a more complex question: should those on government training schemes be added to the current total? This is important because the numbers involved in such programmes today do not have any substantial interwar equivalent. The postwar expansion of public sector employment means that far larger numbers are employed by government now than at any time before the war. Hence it is sometimes hard to distinguish between state-sponsored employment and official training schemes. There is some difficulty in differentiating those employed on a publicly funded urban development programme, for example, and those undertaking similar work on one of the Department of Employment's Employment Training (ET) projects or on the Youth Training Scheme (YTS). The anomaly, however, is an old one. In interwar Britain, those employed on public works projects were not included in the unemployment statistics; those on government 'training' – in Transfer Instruction Centres (TIC) or Juvenile Instruction Centres – were still reliant on official benefits and thus still 'counted' as unemployed. Of course the numbers involved in the 1930s were very small. Only 120,000 passed through the TICs in the full decade of their existence (1928–39). Public expenditure cuts decimated public works programmes in the first half of the decade. However, for the sake of compatibility, those currently on government training and work experience programmes ought to be added to the present-day total of unemployed. In 1986, the numbers involved in schemes like YTS and the Community Programme or in receipt of state sponsorship of some type, stood at 625,000. Thanks to the new government scheme for the long-term unemployed which started in 1987, this number expanded to reach nearly 900,000 two years later.

When these 'trainees' and those falling foul of current benefit regulations are added to those officially recognized as 'unemployed', the total figure for 1986 goes well over the 4 million mark, giving an unemployment rate of over 15 per cent. This exceeds the readjusted rate of 13–14 per cent unemployment in 1932, the worst year of the Slump. Of course, these percentages are only approximations. They do not reflect 'real' levels of unemployment – whatever that may mean – either then or now. The comparison is rather rough, but it does substantiate the statement, made at the beginning of this section, that Margaret Thatcher has presided over the worst unemployment record in our history. Official statistics have disguised this fact. Nonetheless, when historians of the future come to examine the recession of the 1980s, they may well note its similarity to the Slump – arguably in terms of its underlying economic causes, and certainly in terms of its social characteristics – which will be outlined in the following sections.

The distribution of unemployment

There is a case for claiming, therefore, that unemployment in the 1980s has probably been higher than it ever was in the 1930s. Further, the underlying causes of unemployment – notably the collapse of the export industries – are similar. In both the early 1930s and the early 1980s, workers in shipbuilding, iron and steel, textiles, engineering and coal-mining bore the brunt of the recession; then as now, those working in the service sector of the economy remained relatively protected. As a result, regional disparities in the incidence of unemployment have been marked. In both periods, the north-east, the north-west, south Wales, northern Ireland and Scotland experienced rates of unemployment well above the national average. During two world wars this century, government money has poured into these regions. The demand for munitions and transport during the national emergencies gave a new lease of life to the heavy industries located there and effectively postponed the restructuring of local economies away from those old trades where Britain's international performance has long been weak. In the 1980s, however, the west midlands has been added to the list. In the interwar years, this area was relatively prosperous. Today, a line can be drawn from the Bristol Channel to the Wash, with unemployment markedly higher in the northern sector. Around 94 per cent of manufacturing jobs lost between 1979 and 1986 were located there. New industry has settled disproportionately in the south and east, including the recently expanded banking, insurance and financial services.

Within this broad division, unemployment has not been evenly distributed; the problem – both then and now – has been an urban one. In 1986, towns in the depressed regions like Liverpool,

Barnsley, Sunderland, Merthyr, Aberdare, Greenoch and Irvine all had unemployment rates in excess of 20 per cent, with Cookstowne and Strabane in northern Ireland at 36.8 and 38.7 per cent respectively. By contrast, Guildford, Bury St Edmunds, Tunbridge Wells, Slough and Aylesbury all had unemployment rates in the region of 6 per cent.[3] It is worth noting that these differences, although shocking, are not nearly as marked as they were in the 1930s when, at the height of the Slump, unemployment in some towns was over 50 per cent. This improvement is partly attributable to the postwar expansion of the public sector and partly to the effects of past regional policies deliberately designed to diversify local employment in order to prevent the re-emergence of high levels of unemployment resulting from structural imbalances in the national economy.

The other major development since the interwar years lies in the way that inner city unemployment has developed into a racial problem. This aspect of the issue stems partly from the immediate postwar period. Chronic labour shortages led both government and employers to encourage immigration from the so called 'New Commonwealth' to man those jobs too lowly paid to attract white workers. Recent high levels of unemployment among the black communities cannot be attributed to poor linguistic abilities. The majority of current victims were born in Britain or, at least, have lived here for the greater part of their lives. Further, research has shown that fully trained and professional black people have fewer job opportunities commensurate with their qualifications than their white counterparts. So it is not possible to explain the high unemployment among blacks in terms of their lack of skills (unemployment long having been higher among the unskilled than the rest of the labour force). Between 1985 and 1987, unemployment among white males averaged 11 per cent; for the same years the figures were 15 per cent for Indians, 24 per cent for West Indians, 28 per cent for Pakistanis. Although female unemployment rates were lower, these contrasts illustrate a degree of racial discrimination in the job market which explains why black communities in Britain are socially deprived – and why they were at the centre of rioting and violence in Bristol, London, Liverpool and Birmingham in the mid-1980s.

There are other features of the recent crisis that bring the 1930s more to mind. In the early stages of both periods, part-time work proliferated as employers sought to reduce their liabilities in the short term without damaging the possibility of recovery by casting loose workers with skills or experience vital to their business. Such patterns changed as the recession lengthened. A high incidence of long-term unemployment characterizes both eras; indeed, the very notion of 'long term' unemployment developed during the Slump. In this respect, the situation in recent years has definitely been worse than it was before the war. Unemployment in the 1980s remained high for much longer than in the 1930s. In 1986, before the introduction of the Restart and Employment Training initiatives, 1.3 million people had been out of work for more than one year, 800,000 for more than two:[4] roughly treble the number for the 1930s.

A proportion of the long-term unemployed in the 1980s have been young people who have had no 'real' job since leaving school. Like the young unemployed before the war, this group has been the chief target for policies designed to retrain the redundant, to encourage them to move to more prosperous areas. The core of the problem remains among older workers who, as manufacturing contracted, found themselves stranded with unwanted skills in just those parts of the country where opportunities are most limited. Their plight epitomizes the structural nature of the unemployment problem. The demand for labour simply does not match the supply available. Good secretaries, telephone receptionists and office cleaners may be at a premium in central London; this does nothing to help the ex-steel-worker in Consett, who has little inclination and less aptitude for the work involved and who – redundancy pay or no – has not the resources to meet the cost of moving to a more expensive area. This immobility is not helped by the recent growth of owner-occupation in the housing market, or by the moratorium on council house building. Static house prices in depressed areas make it impossible for their owners to consider moving to an area of potential employment where the property market is more buoyant.

Hence older workers fester in their old communities, increasingly unattractive to prospective employers and forming the intractable heart of the unemployment problem. Hardly surprising, therefore, that the Conservative government has tended to understand this group as 'unemployable' and to interpret their situation as 'early retirement'. In so doing, the state is merely following market judgements. Research in the interwar years and in recent times has shown that employers discriminate consistently in favour of young and healthy applicants when recruiting labour and rid themselves of their least productive workers – commonly older men – when faced with a fall in business. Hence, once out of a job, the older worker is liable to have a tough time finding a new position. In similar fashion, those unemployed whose health is poor or who suffer from minor disabilities find it very hard to re-enter the labour market. As recession deepens and the competition for work stiffens, so the discrimination against the disabled moves further and further up the health spectrum of the workforce. Those whose health is not good have recently been 'rationalized' off the labour market in large numbers.[5] In both the early 1980s and the early 1930s, the incidence of 'long-term sickness' among workers rose as economic conditions worsened, demonstrating the 'seepage' of labour market rejects into other categories of social dependency.

The association between age and infirmity has long been reflected in the earnings curve of manual workers – the majority of the workforce until well into this century – which peaked when a man was in his prime and dwindled as old age approached. The earliest state pensions were designed as an annuity to complement falling income; they only became conditional on retirement after the Second World War. In 1881, 73 per cent of British men over the age sixty-five years had a job of some description. A century later, in spite of higher levels of health and lower physical requirements on the job market, only 11 per cent of men in this age group were in work. Before the introduction of state-sponsored retirement, the age at which workers quit their jobs for good depended on both their physical capacities and the degree of competition for work. In periods of high unemployment, 'retirement' has tended to permeate to younger age groups, only to recede again when the demand for labour picks up. In the immediate aftermath of the Second World War, a period of severe labour shortage, social research proved that the health and well-being of the elderly was enhanced if they continued in paid employment. At this time, both government and employers had an interest in persuading workers to postpone retirement. In the 1980s, these findings were conveniently forgotten; all sorts of financial incentives were provided to encourage older men and women to quit work early – to release jobs for the young unemployed. Again, economic, social and political factors combined in different ways in different periods to promote different types of labour market behaviour among older people – and perceptions of retirement changed as a result. We can note that, in the professional sector, individual politicians and judges have prolonged their working lives well after the official retirement age with no apparent ill-effects to themselves or their office. For the less illustrious, advancing age spells inevitable redundancy: even though many now in early retirement (sometimes called long-term unemployment) have never been more capable of working for a living.

While policy-makers regard unemployment among older workers as inevitable, among the young it is seen not merely as undesirable but as positively immoral. The 1987 initiative for the long-term unemployed, Restart, was designed with the under twenty-five-year-old in mind. Since the mid-1970s at least, young people in general, school leavers in particular, have formed the main target for state unemployment policies. After a decade of public training and employment programmes, identified by a constantly changing series of initials, an OECD survey in 1986 found that unemployment rates among the under twenty-four age group still stood at 22 per cent, a figure well above the national average.[6] Thanks to the propensity for YOP, YTS and CP to concentrate on teenagers, the problem has been particularly pronounced among the 20–24 age group. Those who left school at the beginning of the 1980s had a tough time; unemployment was rising rapidly and employers had ceased to take on new recruits. Many never had the chance of a 'real' job, but eked out a precarious existence, moving from scheme to state benefits and back again. In the late 1980s, efforts were made to increase the mobility of this group. Benefit was disallowed to those who failed to move in search of work after ten weeks and the introduction of the community charge (better known as the 'poll tax') in replacement of the rates, places an obligation on parents to pay for adult children living at home. Such penalties help to raise the numbers of homeless among the young and single.

Certainly, a rising incidence of vagrancy characterizes both the 1930s and the 1980s; many took to the road in search of help, subsequently losing their bearings and social orientation. Once again, those sleeping rough are not classified as 'unemployed'; nor is their predicament attributed to economic recession.

Much recent social research has understood youth unemployment as a late twentieth-century problem. Certainly, if we confine our attention to school leavers alone, it is hard to find any exact precedent for the interwar years. Before the Second World War, however, young people entered the labour market at fourteen years of age; juniors in 'boy' jobs earned lower wages than their seniors. Once old enough to command an adult rate, they frequently found themselves turned out of work in favour of a new generation of school leavers. Although the comparative cheapness of teenage labour made such practices attractive, there was a high incidence of unemployment among the 'older young' whose lack of marketable skills pushed them into an already overstocked pool of general labourers. Public concern for their future was high. Then as now, commentators and social analysts expressed fears about what was then referred to as the 'demoralization' of the young: that they would become disillusioned and would 'settle' to a life on the dole. The association between youth unemployment and rising crime rates, although unsupportable under close examination, added to the time-honoured association between unemployment and the collapse of common social values. For very similar reasons, therefore, interwar unemployment policies also focused on the plight of the young worker, whose access to benefit was restricted and who was the chief target of such training programmes as existed at that time.[7]

Even so, it would be wrong to suggest that the scale of youth unemployment during the Slump was anywhere near as severe as it has been in recent times. Two principal reasons can be given to explain the change. In the first place, the aftermath of the Second World War witnessed the raising of the school leaving age, the arrival of full employment and the spread of free collective bargaining, all of which helped eradicate the differential between adult and juvenile wages – thereby removing the competitive edge school leavers had as a source of cheap labour. Secondly, since the 1960s, greater job security among the established workforce encouraged employers to reduce labour costs through a process of 'natural wastage' as an alternative to radical restructuring and mass redundancies. This effectively placed a moratorium on new recruitment, damaging the chances of those starting work for the first time. Recent initiatives to alleviate their plight have focused on reducing the cost of employing young people, through subsidized training schemes and by removing statutory controls over minimum rates of pay for this age group. Such strategies obviously distort official figures on 'real' unemployment in this sector, while simultaneously shifting the problem on to the 'older young' in a manner highly reminiscent of the interwar period.

From the varying treatment afforded the old, the physically impaired, the vagrant and the young, we see that not all those seeking work are automatically classified as 'unemployed'. Changing economic and social pressures influence the categorization of social dependency. This becomes particularly clear when we consider the question of gender, which is central to this issue. Half the population of working age is female, but politicians, statisticians and economists alike have dithered endlessly over whether a woman – particularly a married woman – can be labelled 'unemployed'. Currently, the possession of a marriage certificate is not central in determining the answer to this question. If a woman is cohabiting with a man (that is, if a man spends two nights a week at her house) then she has no right to income support in supplement to her unemployment benefit and loses all right to state support once that benefit is ended (after six months). If a woman is living in celibacy and isolation, but is caring for children or other dependent(s), she may easily fall foul of the 'availability for work' regulation and will not be classified as 'unemployed'. And if a woman has only been in part-time employment (redefined in 1988 as twenty-seven hours a week or less) – and there has been a marked increase in part-time female workers during the 1980s – she will have no access to benefit as of right anyway and her inclusion in the unemployment figures will be determined by her sexual relationships, domiciliary arrangements and the numbers and ages of her offspring . . . everything, that is to say, except her past work record and her desire to find a new job. The postwar period may have witnessed a revolution in female participation in the labour force but the acceptance of female unemployment has lagged well behind.

The reasons underpinning the very different treatment given to women who lose their jobs are rooted in age-old assumptions about the family as the central agency of mutual support. This has nothing to do with changes in the demand for labour and everything to do with our cultural heritage and the political attitudes stemming from it. For over a hundred and fifty years, the debate over the status and significance of women's 'work' has continued. Because much of this work has been home-based, and done in exchange for goods and services as well as wages, it has often been held to be of inferior value to that of the male 'breadwinner'. Even the decennial census provides a very partial view of female economic activity rates. It seriously underestimates the numbers of women who, before the Second World War, took in mending, laundry, or lodgers, took up child-minding, went charring, sold home produce or worked in a variety of ways to earn money to make ends meet. At the more formal end of the market, we do know that, thanks to the mechanization of housework and the advent of reliable contraception, the proportion of married women workers has increased substantially since the Second World War. In 1921, fewer than 10 per cent of married women were in formal paid employment; by 1986, this figure had risen to over 50 per cent. Of course, many of these are in the very part-time jobs that would have escaped the notice of the census enumerator in 1921; the expansion largely reflects the growth in the market provision of local services. In terms of the measurement of female unemployment, however, the 1930s and 1980s are equally unsatisfactory. In the 1930s, steps were taken to restrict access by married women to official unemployment relief, which meant they tended not to register at the employment exchanges and were not included in the official statistics. As a result, we do not have official data which tells us very much about female 'unemployment' at all.

When all these factors are taken into account, the concept of unemployment takes on a very fluid, amoebic quality. Contrary to our common assumptions, the term cannot be taken to refer to all those seeking work, nor to all those thrown out of work as the result of a recession. The prevailing demand for labour encourages definitions of the labour market itself to change, in both a formal and informal way. The workforce has been defined in part by statutory regulation, in part by social custom and industrial practice. In terms of the latter criteria, we can observe how other categories of social dependency absorb a proportion of those thrown out of work by recession. Our notions of who is to be given priority in the apportionment of jobs has not been constant. Criteria of 'unemployability' have fluctuated in a similar fashion; those deemed physically, mentally or socially incapable of work in one era have been incorporated into the job market in another. This invites the conclusion that unemployment is defined by social and political factors just as much as by economic ones and is a perspective that will be developed further in later chapters.

Unemployment: the social problem

We might question whether high levels of unemployment matter very much any more. The unemployed get better social security benefits today than they did in the 1930s and, some would claim, the expansion of the welfare state since that time has generally increased the well-being of the very poor. If we look at the situation with the cool detachment of some economists, unemployment could be seen as positively beneficial. High unemployment has increased the competition for jobs; this has contained industrial militancy and reduced both the political power and the numerical strength of the trade union movement. Such developments, some argue, were vital for the restoration of managerial prerogative and the efficient running of British industry. Industrial restructuring was long overdue and higher unemployment has been the price British society has had to pay for decades of policies which ignored the laws of the market. Unemployment is thus a sign of a healthy economy, with business adopting new technology and production techniques, unconstrained by overmanning and those restrictive practices traditionally imposed by organized labour to protect jobs.

Then there is the problem of inflation. In the mid-1970s, unemployment and prices were rising together; the aim of the Thatcher administrations of the 1980s was to contain the threat of inflation. This would restore faith in the British economy, a vital step towards the solution of the unemployment problem. Higher rates of joblessness might be the unfortunate, but inevitable, outcome of this process, but this effect would be temporary. Unemployment, in any case, might be understood as a minority problem. Inflation, on the other hand, threatens the whole community. It erodes the value of personal savings and hurts those on fixed incomes, particularly pensioners. It encourages short-term speculation at the expense of long-term investment, undermines good industrial relations, reduces confidence in the pound sterling and thus damages Britain's standing on the international money markets. It therefore threatens free enterprise and those traditional social values – personal thrift, hard work, self-reliance – that are commonly understood to be fundamental to economic revival and general prosperity. If inflation were contained, investment would be encouraged and 'real' jobs would be secured.

This, in brief, is a view that became common in the 1980s and helped to return Margaret Thatcher to office in two general elections that decade. It is, however, an oversimplified view. It overlooks the broader implications of the situation: the way, in other words, that unemployment generates its own indirect costs. Unemployment is associated with unpleasant social consequences, and, one way or another, these are translated into higher rates of social expenditure. Counting the cost of high unemployment is not only a matter of adding together the amount spent (on social security) and the revenue foregone (lost taxes). The unemployed show a propensity for alcohol and drugs. Their marriages are more likely to fail; their children more liable to suffer from low birth weight, poor health, low educational achievement. Homelessness is particularly high among the single unemployed. There is also the more general question: whether unemployment creates unemployability – and thus permanent social dependency. Research shows that rising levels of unemployment are closely associated with higher rates of physical and mental sickness. A higher incidence of crime has become the hallmark of many inner cities. Although it may be hard to prove that unemployment is the sole cause of these problems, the fact that their incidence is rising – and rising fastest in areas of high unemployment – indicates, at the very least, that a society suffering from unemployment is liable to suffer from other social maladies, which spells a growing burden for public expenditure, especially on the police, social security and the social services.

All this caught the Conservative government unawares in the early 1980s. As a result, levels of domestic expenditure remained high; attempts to meet an old electoral commitment to reduce levels of taxation had to be postponed until later in the decade. Once again, it is tempting to make comparisons with the 1930s; at that time, governments also found that levels of social expenditure rose inexorably, in spite of every official attempt to contain them. The Thatcher government is not the first to be taken unawares by the broader financial consequences of high unemployment. However, when trying to decide whether a high degree of joblessness is socially tolerable, we should not allow our judgement to be based on economic factors alone. The issue has generated a great deal of interest in the broad social and political consequences in their own right, which raise questions of justice and the rights of citizens living in what purports to be a civilized society. In other words, the experience of unemployment – and the toll it takes from its victims – must also enter into our consideration before we can decide whether unemployment is tolerable at its present level.

As in the 1930s, high unemployment has provoked a sustained interest among social scientists. Numerous teams of investigators have set out for the black spots, to monitor and measure the effects of unemployment on its victims and their families. Reams of reports have been produced; these attempt to give moral outrage some sound statistical foundations. No one could doubt that the families of the unemployed are among the most disadvantaged in the country. Their problems are largely, although not totally, the problems of poverty. Unlike other long-term claimants, the unemployed who have been out of work for a prolonged period are not allowed to claim the higher rate of income support. Justified as a means of pushing the most recalcitrant back into work, all this does is to exacerbate an existing tendency toward debt, defaults on hire-purchase repayments, mortgage arrears and so on. The most desperate are driven into the hands of the loan sharks, or towards illegal activity, raising the costs of surveillance for the authorities. Nor is poverty simply due to reduced household income. The unemployed find daily expenditure increases because they have lost not only a job but also access to the firm's subsidized canteen. The loss of a set of working overalls means that personal clothes wear out that much more quickly. The cost of keeping the home warm all day adds to fuel bills. In the longer term, the picture is even more bleak. Thanks to the recent privatization of social welfare, the unemployed lose not only their present wages but also damage – even lose – their right to superannuation, especially if their previous employer has gone into liquidation. In this way, future income is forfeit and dependence on state social security is prolonged into old age.

A long period of means-tested benefits uses up savings and other resources, as the experience of the 1930s should have taught us. An ex-miner from Caerphilly recalled the effects of the notorious household means test during the Slump:

> If someone had a decent home, the man from the Means Test came and made a list of what you had. Then you were told to sell a wardrobe this week, some chairs next week, some pictures the week after, until you perhaps only had your bed, two chairs and a table left. Only then would you be able to claim something.[8]

Arguably, income support is administered a little more leniently than this. However, the advent of the Social Fund (which forces claimants to repay what are now loans for the replacement of essential items) may well stimulate similar sorts of deprivation among families forced to take desperate measures to make ends meet.

Over and above the general problem of poverty lies the stigma associated with unemployment. This adds to the stress of job loss and the disorientation consequent on the sudden lack of formal structure in the individual's day-to-day life. Compulsory idleness can lead to despair, self-hatred, pessimism. Stress manifests itself in a variety of ways, ranging from mental depression to marital breakdown. Our social values emphasize the importance of self-reliance, the ability to earn one's own living independent of charitable or state support. This is reflected in – and reinforced by – public policy; there are ways in which full-time workers are rewarded while those who are economically inactive are not. The whole notion of contributory state insurance, for example, is premissed on the idea that those who work regularly and accrue the requisite number of contributions should be able to claim help from the state as of right. The economically inactive are offered no such privileges. The incentive for married women to take waged work has been increased by this and by a variety of other incentives (for example, the recent changes in the divorce laws which now mean that no woman can claim maintenance from her ex-husband in her own right). Indeed, the status of being 'employed' is now so marked that women who are 'only housewives' feel stigmatized and degraded by their position. In the 1980s, when the labour market was desperately overcrowded, these factors were encouraging people to seek employment in increasing numbers.

Overall, the unemployed army appears a demoralized lot. Unlike the years of the Slump, the 1980s have not witnessed the active organization of the unemployed as a political force. There is no present-day substitute for the National Unemployed Workers' Movement and, aside from one or two Right to Work marches in the early 1980s, no equivalent to the hunger marches of 1932, 1934 and the Jarrow march of 1936. Quite why this should be the case is hard to explain. Arguably, higher densities of unemployment in the 'depressed areas' before the war encouraged workers in the provinces to organize against the locally administered means test. Possibly the greater experience of hunger provoked more extreme political responses. Certainly, the enormous expansion of a more sophisticated media in recent years has fostered a greater uniformity of political perspective, obscuring local convictions about the rights due to unemployed people. Finally, no coherent alternative policy proposals have been developed of late which offer a way out of the present dilemma. In the 1930s, J. M. Keynes published his treatise on demand management as the means to eradicate unemployment. The Labour Party was developing its strategies for managing the economy, using central state planning and the nationalization of industry as the means to full employment and national prosperity. There were alternatives and this encouraged political purpose, if not among the unemployed themselves, then certainly among their sympathizers. This is no longer the case today.

These differences can be exaggerated; then as now, the vast majority of the unemployed were characterized by their apathy and sense of hopelessness. The following account of a semi-skilled engineer from Coventry shows how unemployment takes its toll.

> I used to get up at 6 a.m., like I was going to work. I thought I would get a job in a couple of weeks, but now it's a couple of years. That's frightening, my confidence is going. When people ask me how long I have been out of work, I think, shall I lie? When you're unemployed, you feel like you have committed a crime somewhere but nobody tells you what you have done. . . . Sometimes I think I'll go barmy. Of course you get depressed, you convince yourself it's you.
>
> I used to eat steak and things, and a chop, tomato and bread and butter. Dead easy. First I went down to bacon sandwiches, now it's just sandwiches. . . . I've bought no new clothes since I was made redundant.[9]

Poverty feeds depression because it forces inactivity; even going down the pub for a pint requires money. Thus the unemployed are pushed out of social life as well as losing workplace contacts and friendships. 'I never go out, never see any friends' is a frequently repeated phrase. And for those men whose wives are earning a wage in their own right, matters are made worse by enforced dependency:

> After a year the dole ran out then I had a year of no money at all, because my wife was working. That was totally unfair for my wife. I wasn't regarded as an individual by society, I was just an appendage, which was sickening. If I wanted to go anywhere I had to scrounge from the wife . . . which was disgraceful. Of course it makes you narky. I've met one or two lads in the town and there was one or two cases where the lads were hopping mad – one of them solved the problem by agreeing to part so he was able to claim for himself. . . . it cost the state much more because housing had to be found for him, as well as income.[10]

Feminists might argue that these unemployed men are not experiencing anything that redundant working wives had not gone through for years. Even so, the operation of the social security regulations adds to the strains male unemployment imposes on a marriage. For men, unlike women, unemployment means feeling totally superfluous, without use or purpose. This aspect of unemployment has remained pretty timeless in its effects; the interwar social investigators turned up very similar evidence.

In short, economic arguments as to whether free labour markets 'clear' or whether state expenditure can promote economic growth without raising inflation provide too narrow a perspective on unemployment, which is as much a social problem as an economic one. Moreover, the desire to divorce economic from social factors influencing the distribution of work or the shaping of public policy is unrealistic. The history of British economic policy since the war is replete with instances of governments bowing to political pressures in preference to the priorities indicated by prevailing economic theories, pumping money destined for new industries into maintaining jobs in old ones and so on. Political demands and social forces use different economic justifications to promote specific strategies. The development of policies for the unemployed illustrates this repeatedly. For example, before the First World War, public works for the unemployed aimed to help married men with families to support. In contemporary economic terms, this made sense. These men were expensive to maintain on public relief. Their experience made them more productive workers; their responsibilities gave them the motivation to work steadily, while their necessarily high levels of expenditure helped stimulate local goods and services. Now traditional practices are quite reversed. Today, the teenage unemployed are the target groups for state-sponsored employment and training. This preference is justified in terms of preventing long-term social dependency and investing in the nation's future. Both economic justifications are perfectly respectable. What has changed, however, is the way unemployment is constructed and how it is visualized as a political problem. Changing perceptions and political pressures have redefined public priorities, and the economic justifications underpinning policy.

This is not to argue that present-day social research necessarily promotes a better understanding. Most sociological effort has been directed towards surveying the unemployed and their households. Somehow it is assumed that quantifying the characteristics of the unemployed will reveal the cause of their common complaint, as well as the consequences unemployment inflicts on its victims. The result is an analysis of unemployment couched in terms of individual disadvantage or inadequacy. This invites initiatives to rectify matters by improving individual performance: the perfection of self-presentation at job interview or the raising of employment-related skills. This perspective justifies policies which redistribute unemployment – by promoting the chances of one applicant at the expense of the rest. The cynic might observe that such strategies can be used to shift unemployment away from politically volatile groups and towards those whose joblessness could be redefined as 'early retirement' or 'economic inactivity'. Structural factors explaining the incidence and nature of unemployment are all but ignored. Any historical understanding which might help put both the present crisis and political responses to it in a broader perspective is similarly neglected. The Second World War forms an historical benchmark beyond which current understanding does not run. This has led to the impression that high levels of joblessness are abnormal because they are unprecedented, at least within the memory of those now studying the problem and policy responses to it. What was 'normal' in the past, whether 'unemployment' was a problem, is lost in a haze of vague impressions. The remainder of this book will be dedicated to clearing the air.

II

Historical Perspectives

Introduction

It is hard to superimpose the twentieth-century notion of unemployment on the mid-nineteenth-century labour market. There are no statistics, national or otherwise. Patterns of work were very diverse, varying not only between different industries and trades but also within the same industry in different parts of the country. It was possible to find workers ostensibly in full-time work, like outworkers in clothing or tailoring, in a state of semi-starvation, while others, such as coal or deal porters on the docks, had no regular job but were well paid enough to avoid poverty. Further, similar industries managed manpower in different ways in different areas. In the coal industry, for example, Durham miners were until 1844 'bound' annually to their employers and were payed a fixed weekly wage; south Wales miners, by contrast, shared work when times were hard, working short-time on reduced earnings. Indeed, short-time was a common response to falling demand in a number of industries, particularly textiles and mining. It allowed employers to hold on to experienced hands while affording some sort of income to workers who otherwise might be left destitute. Similarly, the large number of workers who were paid by the piece could easily lose work because the demand for their product had declined, without becoming totally redundant. Segregating the 'unemployed' from the rest of the labour force becomes a more or less impossible task; the problem was really one of underemployment among many rather than unemployment among few.

The enormous variation in the nature of waged work is not the only difficulty here. The separation of a 'labour force' from the rest of the population is also problematic. The pre-industrial economy centred primarily on the household; every member physically capable of making a contribution was expected to do so. This tended to blur the distinction between waged and unwaged work. Industrialization separated work from home and this reduced the wage-earning capacity of married women who were tied down by household duties. It is hard to estimate the economic activity rates of this group, but at the end of the eighteenth century it seems probable that they were similar to those of today, although much less visible because hidden within the home.

The age limits of the working population were determined simply by physical capacity. In the late eighteenth century, children as young as six or eight years old could be found working in the earliest textile mills, as well as in coal-mines and agriculture. As their hardest taskmasters were often their own parents, it is unlikely that industrialization itself introduced children to the world of work at earlier ages than had prevailed before, although the long hours (twelve or fourteen a day) and intensity of effort might well have been more unusual. Statutory attempts to impose restrictions on the use of child labour in the 1830s and 1840s were not successful. Both employers and parents colluded in their evasion, the former because child labour was cheap and more easily disciplined, the latter because children's earnings were vital in the constant battle against poverty. Larger families tended to be poor families and family size grew during the early nineteenth century. The introduction of compulsory education in 1880 was far more effective in eliminating such practices than anything that went before.

Equally, Victorian England did not recognize a common age of retirement from working life, which was determined by the requirements of the job and the physical capacity of the worker concerned. Work was overwhelmingly manual and a premium was placed on physical strength and stamina, which faded with age, especially when accompanied by a poor diet consequent on low earnings. Hence, although far fewer men reached our current age of retirement at sixty-five, earnings and working capacity fell off before then, except for those engaged in more sedentary occupations. As a result, the age at which workers 'retired' varied considerably. In the 1840s, Friedrich Engels was observing how miners, whose working conditions bred chronic illnesses and whose job required a high level of physical fitness, were forced to stop work at 35–45 and rarely lived beyond fifty years of age. At the same time Henry Mayhew documented the case of a seventy-year-old London needlewoman who was refused help by the relieving officer because she was considered fit to earn her own living. In all branches of the labour market advancing years spelt reduced earnings, irregular work and, if death did not intervene, eventual reliance on children, charity or the poor law – as 'aged and infirm'. The very merging of what we would now consider separate categories illustrates how old age and its relationship to working capacity was understood. Years alone were not considered adequate reason for claiming public relief; people only stopped working if they had private means or if they had to. When the demand for labour fell in periods of depression, workers were pushed into 'retirement' at younger ages.

Industrialization and employment

The advent of mechanization and the spread of more specialist forms of agriculture helped change both the nature of work and household structures. In the late eighteenth century, the earning of wages became increasingly important for the survival of working-class families. Money-earning activities became more distinct from the general round of household duties as the market – and the cash nexus – permeated the household economy. The process of manufacture moved outside the home. This transition has never been total. Earlier forms of domestic production, in clothing, toy-making, now even computer services, are still visible today, although the balance has evidently changed. By examining the nature and consequences of this transition, the reasons why unemployment emerged as central to the problem of poverty by the end of the last century become more readily apparent.

The swing away from domestic forms of production can be roughly explained by three contemporaneous developments: the growth of the population, the extension of enclosure and the advent of mechanized manufacture, boosting productivity and fostering the growth of new towns and cities. The population of England and Wales grew by approximately 50 per cent in the latter half of the eighteenth century. It was to quadruple over the next hundred years. This expansion coincided with increasing commercialization of farming and a reduction in the demand for labour. This meant an expansion in the number of landless labourers and hence greater competition for work. As the population explosion started before the industrial revolution, it cannot be explained as a consequence of urbanization. Increasingly, historians have come to view the growth in population as central to explaining the rural distress and underemployment commonly associated with the early nineteenth century.

The enclosure of common lands for private use also had a marked impact on the livelihood of the rural labourer and his family. It resulted in a contraction of resources for many workers and a greater reliance on earnings. An earlier mode of life was recorded by Flora Thompson, recalling conversations with an old lady in the 1890s, whose grandfather had built a house for his family on the common ground of their village:

> Country people had not been so poor when Sally was a girl, or their position so hopeless. Sally's father had kept a cow, geese, poultry, pigs and a donkey cart to carry his produce to the market town. He could do this because he had commoners' rights and could turn his animals out to graze and cut furze for firing and even turf to make a lawn for one of his customers. Her mother made butter, for themselves and to sell, baked their own bread and made candles for lighting . . .
>
> Sometimes her father would do a day's work for wages, thatching a rick, cutting and laying a hedge, or helping with the shearing or the harvest. This provided them with ready money for boots and clothes; for food they relied almost entirely on home produce . . .
>
> Everybody worked; the father and mother from daybreak to dark. Sally's job was to mind the cow and drive the geese to the best grass patches.[1]

The loss of those commoners' rights turned 'the once self-supporting cottager' in George Bourne's words 'into a spender of money at the baker's, the coal merchant's, the provision dealer's; and, of course, needing to spend money, he needed first to get it.'[2] In this way, the spread of enclosure – discernible since the sixteenth century – pushed rural labourers, their wives and children, on to the labour market in a search for work which was made the more frenzied by falling farm prices (and wages) in the aftermath of the Napoleonic wars.

These developments coincided with the advent of factory-based textile production, which itself had a profound impact on the other source of earned income for rural workers: outwork. Different parts of the country had long been associated with different types of product: lace-making around Nottingham, stocking-knitting in Leicester, spinning and weaving of cotton and wool in Lancashire and the West Riding. The appearance of the mills damaged the status and security of some very skilled branches of outwork. Many rural households found themselves thrown into poverty as such work became increasingly scarce or only available at pitifully low rates of pay. The fate of the hand-loom weavers, stocking-frame knitters and silk weavers in the 1830s and 1840s, all reflected the impact of technological change on the distribution of work. Textiles were not the only industry to experience such structural shifts. In town and country alike, mechanization had a marked impact on a wide variety of employment. The position of some skilled workers was undermined while the demand for new skills grew.

The result of the growth in labour supply and agricultural depression was the collapse of farm service in the south and east of the country. It had been customary for farm workers to be hired by the year, to enter service in another household and to live with another family, receiving food, clothes, board and a small annual wage in return for work, only living out when they wished to marry. Children were first put into service at about fourteen years of age, in arrangements commonly lasting about seven years. By the 1780s, however, 'living out' was becoming far more widespread as seasonality of employment increased, notably in the south and east where little alternative employment was available for rural workers. Boys at least came to live with their biological parents for far longer periods in the course of the nineteenth century. This imposed a further burden on already dwindling resources. Not only factory children were open to exploitation at the hands of their employers. Joseph Arch, founder of the National Agricultural Labourers' Union, was first employed as a boy in the 1830s as a human scarecrow at 4d (1.66p) for a twelve-hour day; the farmer beat him if he dared to leave the field. As 'living in' declined, children were competing with grown men for available jobs. For country girls, departure from the family home to enter service remained widespread right up until the First World War, with domestic service replacing farm service as the principal form of initial employment.

By the middle of the nineteenth century, therefore, agrarian employment in southern and eastern counties was both less regular and much less secure than it had been. Seasonal unemployment was rife, notably in arable farming, and the glut of labour on the market, desperate for any work at any wage, allowed farmers to hire and fire at will. Specialist workers and stockmen might be kept on during poor weather or the slack season while ordinary labourers could expect to be 'laid off' for the duration. Such practices bore particularly hard on the poor, as opportunities of supplementing living standards by other means were few and changes in the administration of the poor laws (described later in this chapter) made it impossible to claim parish relief as of right after the mid-1830s. The results were visible in the appearance of gangs of women and children working the fields in all weathers for minimal wages, under the surveillance of overseers in the 1820s and 1830s; visible in the outbursts of incendiarism and rural protest which greeted the introduction of threshing machines, seed drills and other farm machinery in East Anglia in the following decades; and visible in the drift of workers from some rural areas towards the new industrial towns. In northern counties, annual hirings in rural employment remained commonplace.

Urban workers had always been more reliant on the cash nexus than had their rural counterparts. Pre-industrial towns had tended to be commercial centres rather than centres of manufacture; employment there had been characterized by a greater degree of specialization than prevailed elsewhere. Small units of production, providing local goods and services rather than commodities for export, operated largely on a domestic basis. Since the middle ages, craft guilds had governed particular trades in particular towns, stipulating modes of recruitment and training. They were empowered by law to recognize legitimate traders and to punish those who ignored their rules, thus founding a vocabulary concerning the rights of 'legal' men who worked in 'legal' shops which permeated the craft unions in the nineteenth century.

The Elizabethan Statute of Artificers, which provided the legal framework of craft regulation, fell into abeyance long before it was formally repealed in 1811. Under the old system of apprenticeship, the pupil had been formally indentured at fourteen–sixteen years of age and joined the master's house for a period traditionally specified as seven years before being recognized as a journeyman, qualified to practise the trade. It was also usual for journeymen to 'live in', entitled to bed, board and wages in return for their work, only moving out on marriage. Although 'living in' could still be found in small communities in the late nineteenth century, the household structure underpinning such arrangements was starting to disappear a century earlier. From 1790, fewer apprentices were completing their indentures and journeymen's wages were falling, both signs that employers were no longer bothered about hiring only men who had served their time. In the early nineteenth century, the figure of the 'tramping artisan' became more common than it had ever been before as journeymen, usually newly qualified, took to the road, in part to extend their experience and knowledge of their trade, but also to escape increasingly uncertain employment prospects in their immediate locality.

The nature of training for skilled work changed; apprenticeships were shortened and concentrated on specific skills rather than on an extensive understanding of all aspects of production. Lads worked alongside journeymen rather than being attached to a master's household. There were various adverse consequences. The new system bore heavily on apprentices' families, who frequently still paid for indentures while the apprentice lived at home and could expect little or no remuneration for his efforts until his time was served. As the old stipulated ratios between journeymen and boys were increasingly ignored, apprentices became a cheap alternative to adult labour. Such developments were resented by the very journeymen expected to train the new recruits, souring relations and not making for co-operative training. At worst, this became nominal and the fate of the boys was instant dismissal as soon as they were old enough to command an adult rate. Such practices were more common when times were hard. This abuse of apprenticeship provoked sporadic industrial disputes towards the end of the century, as skilled men tried to protect their position and to prevent their trade being flooded by excess labour. For some, the label 'apprentice' became purely nominal, its owner being indistinguishable from the mass of boy labour thronging major urban areas, liable to instant unemployment on reaching adulthood.

At the same time, new mechanized processes facilitated cheaper forms of bulk production. As a result, the market became saturated with semi-skilled workers, who knew something of the trade, but who did not possess the full range of skills expected of the qualified man. Henry Mayhew, chronicling London's labour market in the 1840s, continually contrasted the position of the 'honourable' tradesman – cabinet-maker, tailor, shoe-maker, hatter and so on – with the 'slop' worker whose wages and product undercut old recognized prices and reduced the job security long assumed to belong to the man with an established craft.

The most obvious impact of industrialization was found in the more intense and strictly disciplined nature of work in those industries transformed by the new technology: textiles, coal-mining, metal-processing and engineering. The earliest mills were manned by convict and pauper labour (mostly children) because the regularity of work was alien to an adult population used to a greater degree of autonomy in conducting their working lives. The higher wages available in the factories provided insufficient compensation for the loss of this 'freedom'. Impoverished hand-loom weavers, struggling desperately to make ends meet, would send their daughters to work on the power looms but resisted the prospect themselves. This was as true for Dundee linen weavers in the 1890s as it had been for the woollen cloth weavers in the West Riding half a century earlier. There was a tendency to despise the factory hand as a drudge, a slave to the machine. It was only as pre-industrial forms of work, with their feast days and holidays and their reverence for St Monday, faded from direct memory that routine and regulated work practices became more widely accepted. While the fourteen-hour day imposed by the earliest mills may now seem unduly harsh, it was probably no longer than that found in London's indoor trades in the early seventeenth century. What made it far less acceptable to contemporaries was the mind-crushing tedium of the work involved, the loss of public feast days and holidays and, for middle class observers, the physical consequences of long hours and appalling conditions manifest in the factory towns.

Most early factory operatives were women and children. The association between textile production and women's work was an old one – as the term 'spinster' shows – and we can assume that, under the domestic system, children were also expected to earn their keep. As late at 1851, only half the women recorded by the census as being employed in textile production were factory workers (and twice as many were working as domestic servants). However, the use of female labour in factory or mine was increasingly regarded as wrong. Married women working in the mills neglected their domestic duties and took jobs away from their menfolk, while unmarried girls in pit or factory had no chance to acquire vital domestic skills and were prey to sexual licence and immoral influence. Behind this rhetoric, we can observe how new social norms redefined these jobs as belonging to adult men. It is no coincidence that such concerns became more widespread when recession struck the textile trade. Middle-class organizations sought to impose statutory constraints on the hours and conditions of women's and children's employment in the 1830s and 1840s, supported by workers' organizations who saw such reforms as a means of shortening the hours and improving the employment prospects of working men.

It is very hard to assess the extent of unemployment consequent on cyclical factors in the early nineteenth century. From the figures compiled by local relief committees, it appears that fluctuations in trade in this period hit industrial communities much harder than any before or since. The slump in 1841–2 was particularly brutal in its effects. In Bolton, an estimated 60 per cent of mill-workers were laid off. In Liverpool, between 50 and 75 per cent of building workers and 50 per cent of labourers were getting less than two days work a week. In Dundee, 50 per cent of engineers and shipbuilders were idle. In Leeds and Nottingham, one in five of the population was pauperized; in Clitheroe, 2,300 out of a total population of

6,700 were reliant on poor relief. The ironfounders' union, one of the few to give unemployment relief to its members at this early a date, recorded a rate of 18.5 per cent unemployed in 1841 – and only the best paid and most regularly employed workers were union men. The depression did not follow a period of buoyant trade – the cotton industry had been depressed since 1837 – nor did the ensuing years witness an instant recovery. The slump of 1847 was nearly as bad: in some places arguably worse. The results of recession were manifest in the growth of Chartism and other forms of political radicalism among working-class communities at this time.

The results of cyclical fluctuation was not just felt in the factories; distress was at its most acute where mechanization had had least impact. It hastened the demise of domestic-based wool manufacture – notably in areas like East Anglia and the west country, which found themselves unable to compete any longer with the power-driven mills of the north. In this way, fluctuations in trade hit hardest communities which had been struggling for decades. Manchester alone still contained 50,000 hand-loom weavers in 1837, many of them Irish immigrants, before the depression in trade set in. For communities overwhelmingly reliant on one industry, there was no alternative employment. In the early 1860s, the Lancashire mills again ground to a halt because the American Civil War had cut off their supply of raw cotton. The resulting widespread distress forced both local authorities and charity to improvise in creating work for the operatives in order to forestall further unrest.

The growth of major commercial cities fostered the sort of labour market conditions where it was quite impossible to make clear distinctions between the employed, the unemployed, the self-employed and the economically inactive. Until the middle of the century at least, most of the British population lived in rural areas or small towns of under 50,000 people. The growth of major conurbations came later. As early as 1840, however, London's overstocked labour market, coupled with a highly seasonal demand for goods and services, had produced a degree of casual employment quite unmatched anywhere else. Although still a manufacturing centre at this date, most of the capital's industries were in decline. Shipbuilding on the Thames was to give way to shipyards on the Tyne, the Mersey, the Clyde; the mechanization of silk-weaving in Coventry and Derby, coupled with competition from France, was reducing the skilled weavers in Spitalfields to abject poverty. Employment was becoming increasingly dominated by London's position as a commercial and social centre, which meant it suffered from extreme seasonality. A multiplicity of employers of small-scale enterprise, aided by the over-supply of labour, hired and fired as the needs of their businesses dictated. Mayhew observed at this time:

> Constant employment and consequently constant wages are gradually passing into casual labour and therefore casual earnings; for the economy of labour is daily teaching capitalists to employ their labour only when they are wanted and to get rid of them immediately the business in any way declines; and as most trades are 'brisk' and 'slack' at various periods of the year, a large number of workmen are employed only in the busy season and discharged in dull times.[3]

Subcontracting was rife, notably in the clothing industry, where middlemen 'sweated' domestic workers to earn a profit. Women were taken on at below subsistence wages and still had to pay for their own thread, needles and light. The 'slop' end of the fashion and furnishing trades competed frantically for such orders as were available at almost any price. On the docks, in the railway and building yards, casuals gathered in the hope of a couple of days' work. Right at the bottom of the pile, those temporarily or permanently without any formal paymaster eked out an existence as street sellers, scavengers, beggars, hawkers, mud larks, street acrobats, bone and rag pickers, prostitutes and petty thieves, scraping a living by their wits as best they could. The classification of this impoverished host according to their labour market status has proved an insuperable task for social investigators, both at the time and since.

Casualism became more visible towards the end of the century as other cities spread in size. Developments in public transport allowed the respectable and white-collar workers to move out of city centres, where slums housed workers who needed to be near those concerns offering the chance of an odd day's work. Short-term engagements and casual employment were particularly associated with port transport and the construction industries. In both, small firms dominated the market and, when times were hard, the numbers looking for work grew as the number of jobs available dwindled. In such circumstances, the chances of any labourer without contacts were small; casuals tended to dominate the clientele of both charity and the poor law. Writing at the beginning of this century, Robert Tressell described how competition for work in the building trade fostered casualism and a high incidence of underemployment among the operatives:

> Every firm had a certain number of men who were regarded as regular hands . . . when there was any work to do, they got preference over strangers or outsiders. When things were busy, outsiders were taken on temporarily. When the work fell off, these casual hands were the first to be 'stood still.' If it continued to fall off, the old hands were also stood still in order of seniority, the older hands being preferred to strangers – so long, of course, as they were not old in the sense of being aged or inefficient. . . . In good years, the men of all trades, carpenters, bricklayers, plasterers, painters and so on, were able to keep almost regularly at work, except in wet weather . . . [but] [I]t is rare even in good years for one of the casual hands to be employed by one firm for more than one, two, or three months without a break. It is usual for them to put in a month with one firm, then a fortnight with another, then perhaps six weeks somewhere else . . . and often in between there are two or three days or even weeks of enforced idleness. This sort of thing goes on all through spring, summer and autumn.[4]

Similar patterns of employment are still discernible in some branches of the building trade today. At the end of the last century, this type of employment was relatively common for general labourers, of whom there were over 594,000 according to the 1891 census. All round the country – in ship repair yards, gas-works, foundries, the fishing industry, on the docks, in agriculture, land drainage and public works of various types – extra hands were needed when trade was brisk and there were always extra hands available to be taken on. Those familiar with the local job market and who had the right contacts could play the system to their advantage. Charles Booth, investigating the London labour market in the depressed 1880s, found that such labourers did not stick to one industry, but would perhaps work the building sites in spring, go for a spell in the militia or hop-picking in Kent in the summer, revert to the docks for the corn or timber-handling season and seek work at the gas-works in the winter. Such a life was far from secure, but not all casual workers lived constantly in chronic poverty. Indeed, some preferred the 'freedom' to sell their labour as their needs might dictate to the stolid, routine existence offered by permanent employment. Eleanor Rathbone observed about dockers in Liverpool: 'They have adopted the habits of their lives only too well to the condition of their work and are said to prefer long spells of almost continuous work by day or night, followed by two or three days of complete idleness to regular and moderate hours.'[5]

Cargo-handling was extraordinarily hard work and a regular six-day week was probably a physically impossible task. This did not prevent contemporary commentators condemning casuals as idlers, incapable of holding down a regular job: the inefficient element which should be expelled from the labour market if industry was to prosper and the Empire to thrive.

By the end of the century, cyclical depression and an overstocked labour market combined to make insecurity of employment endemic for unskilled workers. Skilled trade unions were returning a higher proportion of their members as unemployed for longer periods than ever before. Competition for work was fierce in every sector of the labour market; urbanization had raised still further general reliance on earnings for survival. There were, however, other reasons why men and women fought tooth and nail for the poorest jobs at the lowest wages. Changes in the system of public relief exercised a powerful effect on the search for work and to these we must now give our attention.

The relief of the poor

The Poor Law Act of 1601, commonly referred to as the old poor law, conferred on each parish a statutory obligation to relieve the destitute. This act, however, did little more than stipulate who had a right to relief, the means by which relief should be financed and the broad conditions under which it could be obtained. Subsequent legislation tinkered with the machine, endowing the parishes with discretionary new powers, but basically let these authorities get on with the job as best they could. As a result, the old poor law was characterized by its heterogeneity. Different types of help were available under different conditions in different parts of the country, according to the nature of the local economy and the political attitudes towards the destitute prevalent within the community. The parish acted, in effect, like a welfare state in miniature; it provided care for the sick and aged, shelter for the homeless and incomes for those unable to earn enough to make ends meet. As it was virtually impossible to isolate the 'unemployed' from other paupers, the vestry had an interest in solving the problems of the local labour market. And, in devising schemes to deal with surplus labour, some parishes initiated experiments similar to those developed later, at national level, as part of a general programme for the unemployed.

One of the main motives for taking such an interest was, then as now, financial. Relief was funded out of the local rates and hence the ratepayers had a vested interest in restoring the independence of paupers who might otherwise remain idle indefinitely at their expense. The original act stated that the 'able-bodied' poor should be set to work – for much the same reasons that American governments have been advocating 'workfare' in recent years – to demonstrate to the community in general and to the destitute in particular that all were expected to labour for their subsistence, even if there was no waged work available. The issue of social and political stability was also significant; regular labour occupied men who might otherwise turn their dissatisfactions to politically radical ends.

By the eighteenth century, a variety of projects had been initiated by parishes, designed to resolve the problems of local labour markets. In a few instances, residential workhouses had been established as working factories, to enable the paupers to contribute to the costs of their own support. In 1722, legislation was passed allowing parishes to contract the management of the poor on a commercial basis, introducing an element of 'privatization'. Under such circumstances, the overseer was free to exploit the labour of the workhouse inmates at will, as both parish and contractor were eager to profit from such ventures. In the following years, futher legislation was proposed to confine the relief of the able-bodied poor to these well-regulated workhouses, which became more common in textile-producing areas in the south and west.

Theory, however, proved far removed from reality; in practice, such schemes failed to live up to expectations. Voluntary incarceration in the workhouse, especially one demanding extensive hours of labour from its inmates, was unattractive to all but the most desperate: to those, that is, quite incapable of earning an independent living. In-house paupers were overwhelmingly made up of the very old, children, the chronic sick and women – unmarried mothers, widows, deserted wives – who were unable to maintain themselves. In general, most effort went towards the provision of foodstuffs, goods and services for the paupers themselves and few became commercially viable. Some, located in textile-producing areas and taking advantage of the large proportion of female inmates, produced spun yarn for local manufacture. In early nineteenth-century Manchester, the large number of child paupers allowed the establishment of a pin factory. However, by this time, the appearance of factory production – and the difficulties experienced by the early entrepreneurs in finding labour to man them – offered an alternative method of setting the poor to work, or at least some of them, by sending pauper children to the cotton mills and to the long hours, strict discipline and punitive tedium found there.

This was not the first attempt to find work for paupers outside the confines of a workhouse. In the seventeenth century, poor rates had occasionally been used to purchase stock to loan to the unemployed, the profit from which, when worked on and sold, would repay – even profit – the parish for its original outlay. Unfortunately, the combination of lax supervision, poor quality labour and, usually, a depressed local market frequently proved fatal. Stock tended to dwindle rather than grow and that particular system fell into abeyance. However, many parishes were still prepared to advance a loan to the destitute worker trying to re-establish himself in business after prolonged absence (due to sickness, for example), enabling him to re-equip with the necessary tools and materials and to establish a foothold in the local market. Such systems of grants and loans are reminiscent of the present-day Enterprise Allowance Scheme which does roughly the same thing but on a national scale. Both were supposed to prevent the unemployed worker and his family becoming permanently dependent on public funds; both were viewed as viable ways of extending the number of jobs available in the local community. Both have been subsequently criticized as potentially counterproductive. Such enterprises, their critics claim, threaten to undermine the viability of existing independent concerns because they subsidize the less efficient worker, enabling him to undercut his more efficient colleague. Thanks to the subsidy, they arguably destroy as many jobs as they might create.

Many parishes were keen for pauper children to become financially independent as soon as possible. Rate moneys were used to pay for apprenticeships in an established trade. In Bristol, for example, city apprentices in printing were even enfranchised on the completion of their indentures. For the poor law was not alone in providing such training. All around the country, innumerable local bequests and charities operated to fund schools and apprenticeships for the poor, with the object of helping them to become self-supporting. At the end of the eighteenth century, the rising numbers of paupers and the competition for such places hastened the decline in the 'training' element of pauper apprenticeships. These deteriorated to become little more than a device for ridding the parish of poor children, in many instances amounting to a simple system of 'boarding out' in households prepared to offer basic shelter in return for the child's labour and a small stipend from the rates. Others appear to modern eyes more like a residential form of the YTS. Training was left in the hands of the contracting employer. The children who manned the early cotton mills and worked in the expanding coal industry were often pauper apprentices. Girls were 'apprenticed' into domestic service, usually the least desirable positions; boys were sent into the armed forces – particularly the navy and the merchant marine. The placement of the young continued to be a priority in the work of the poor law authorities throughout the following century. All too often, pauper children were the most abused child labour, working long hours in 'sweated' trades for a pittance of a wage. Their 'training' lay less in the acquisition of marketable skills than in their adaptation to a life of drudgery.

As destitution increased in the late eighteenth century, notably in the overstocked labour markets of the rural south, other strategies were developed to put the poor to work. Under the 'roundsmen' system, unemployed labourers were required to visit local farmers in search of work, who, in their turn, were obliged to pay a supplementary poor rate if they failed to take on a stipulated number of such applicants. In most instances, the wages of pauper labourers were supplemented by the parish; this reviled system of 'relief in aid of wages' was the chief target of the old poor law's critics in 1832. In a manner similar to the publicly subsidized work experience schemes of the 1970s, employers were being provided with a strong financial incentive to take on extra hands – only, then as now, critics argued that these were rarely additional workers, but replaced those whose wages the employer would otherwise have to find out of his own pocket. Later in the nineteenth century, under the 'ticket' system, poor law claimants had to prove their availability for work by undergoing a similar search, but being denied any support from the rates if taken on. Under both systems, local guardians demanded proof of the applicant's willingness to work – any work at any wages – before granting relief. The requirement that the unemployed should be genuinely seeking work before being given state help has a venerable history.

Before the reforms in 1834, lost income resulting from the spread of enclosure, the decline of outwork and the changes in agricultural management was in part recompensed by parish relief. By the 1790s, many parishes in the south of the country had established scales of relief, allowing payment to be determined according to household size and the prevailing price of bread. This made it a sort of index-linked system of family support (as the old family income supplement was renamed in April 1988), although a reasonably generous one. Relief was usually distributed in the form of loaves of bread, or the equivalent in flour. Commonly referred to as the Speenhamland system, after the area in Berkshire where these scales were enforced by order of the local magistrate, poor law relief thus operated to help employed and unemployed alike. Indeed, each parish was effectively a local Department of Social Security (DSS), applying its own regulations to provide pensions for the elderly, compensation for lost earning capacity and protecting the poor from both the loss of work and the effects of inflation on low wages. In a period characterized by economic fluctuation and instability of employment, the rights of the poor to help from their parish became increasingly important to a wider range of workers, who were liable to be forced back on such relief at some point in their lives. It kept starvation at bay for the impoverished farm workers, and the hand-loom weavers and stockingers displaced by the new factories. And when these rights to communal support were withdrawn, there was uproar, signifying the extent to which the labouring poor had come to rely on poor relief as essential to their survival.

Rising inflation during the Napoleonic wars and chronic agricultural depression in their aftermath caused the cost of the poor law to rise from around £2 million per annum in 1784 to around £6 or £7 million in the 1820s. The consequences of this increase for rate-payers, especially those only marginally above the poverty line themselves, formed a bedrock of discontent and the foundations of a movement for reform. Initial efforts to contain rising costs had been visible since the 1780s. In much the same fashion as the 1986 Social Security Act, parishes reduced – in some cases abolished – what we would now call 'one off' payments for fuel, clothing, shoes, special nursing and so on. Half a century later, however, such relatively minor adjustments were no longer considered sufficient; the whole structure had to be torn down and replaced. In the writings of political economists like Thomas Malthus and David Ricardo, of social commentators like Harriet Martineau, of social investigators like Edwin Chadwick and the Royal Commission of the Poor Laws, the old system stood indicted. Under its aegis, honest enterprise was burdened with high rates, bullied into employing the least efficient workers and undercut by unscrupulous rivals, who used the growing numbers of subsidized pauper apprentices to replace regular labourers and drove legitimate enterprises out of business. Such public subsidies destroyed free enterprise and extended the distress they were designed to alleviate. Relief in aid of wages offered, to all intents and purposes, a guaranteed minimum wage for all which rendered good character and honest endeavour of little account, discouraged providence and thrift, depressed wages and demoralized the poor. To restore the poor to independence which, as one historian has noted, meant complete dependence on waged work, all forms of outdoor relief had to be abolished. Only the destitute willing to enter the workhouse were to receive help. A new central authority was to be appointed in London to eradicate local 'abuses' and promote greater uniformity of practice. An open letter to Edwin Chadwick (the chief architect of the new system) from an admirer, written as the Poor Law (Reform) Act reached the statute book in 1834, captures nicely the justifications used by reformers for introducing a deterrent system to replace a benevolent one:

> I have never known an instance of a labourer of respectable character and diligent habits who was unable to support his family. . . . The proper object of a poor law is to lessen the number as well as the distresses of the poor. To alleviate suffering is only a secondary purpose; to prevent it is the first; and the surest way to effect this end is to compel the labourers to rely upon their own industry; the surest way to defeat it is to facilitate the access to parochial relief and to make the poor-house tempting as a refuge. The dread of going into the house operates as one of the most powerful incentives to industry; the prospect of finding an easy home there is one of the strongest temptations to indolence and vice. A lavish and indiscriminate charity has the effect of making paupers, not relieving them; and I am persuaded it will be found that the poor are most numerous and the worst off in those parishes where the most is spent upon them.[6]

Official help for the unemployed was to be dominated by this type of logic for the next fifty years.

The old poor law in general and relief in aid of wages in particular have long suffered a bad press. This was largely due to the adverse publicity given to 'abuses' by those who wanted to see the system changed. Historians like Sydney and Beatrice Webb, already convinced of the merits of central administration, found in the poor law everything they considered corrupt and inefficient. It is only relatively recently that this judgement has been reappraised and the old poor law has been viewed in a more favourable light.

The old system had its advantages; relief was adapted to suit local labour market conditions, allowing the comparatively cheap maintenance of agricultural labour during the winter months and enabling Lancashire mill-owners to retain a pool of surplus labour to cope with fluctuations in trade. The 'abuses' noted by the critics were concentrated in the south of the country; soaring costs were the consequence – not the cause – of agricultural depression, low wages, rising prices and an overstocked labour market. There is little sign that wages rose when outdoor relief was abolished. On the contrary, the cost of reform fell on the shoulders of the rural poor themselves; the loss of any supplement from the parish reduced yet further standards of living that were already appallingly low and sent the elderly into the workhouses in droves. By relieving the poor in their homes, the old poor law had caused minimal disruption to household circumstances, enabling claimants to maintain a search for work. In the north of the country, where industrial expansion offered alternative jobs, the old system continued to work relatively well. It was cheaper for the ratepayers to provide allowances for impoverished outworkers than to put them and their families in the workhouse as the new law demanded. Moreover, the workhouse was a peculiarly clumsy instrument for dealing with the victims of an industrial recession. The incarceration of large numbers in periods of slump was not only singularly pointless but also very expensive: more liable to raise the rates than reduce them. By sacrificing flexibility, comprehensiveness, local participation and community support in favour of uniformity, professionalism and the principles of a free market economy, Chadwick and his allies stirred up a hornet's nest of opposition which prevented the effective implementation of his precious reforms.

The new poor law was indeed very unpopular and not just among the poor themselves. The cost of the workhouse aside, the reform represented a major intrusion by central government into local affairs, threatening civil liberties and undermining the rights of local dignitaries to spend the rates that they paid in the way they thought best. In this respect, opposition to the London government was similar to that found among colonial Americans on the eve of their revolution. It was, in part, a struggle against the despotism of an alien authority and one which seemed hell-bent on destroying the traditional understanding and mutual obligations which had existed between rulers and ruled in the past, a relationship already under-mined by enclosure, the factory system and the decline of trade regulation. Poor people in Britain, the Tory radical William Cobbett wrote in 1826, were traditionally protected by a poor law which guaranteed 'the right to live in the country of our birth; the right to have a living out of the land in exchange for our labour . . . the right, in case we fell into distress, to have our wants sufficiently relieved . . . whether that distress arose from sickness, from decrepitude, from old age or from inability to find employ-ment'.[7]

Viewing the past as a golden age of social harmony might not be historically exact, but Cobbett reflects the attitudes of those who saw the abolition of the old poor law as an immoral act, unworthy of a civilized, Christian society and as a development that had to be opposed at all costs. Not all members of the ruling classes were converted to the merits of the new social order. Moreover, the implementation of the new act in the industrial north coincided with the severe slumps in trade of the late 1830s and early 1840s. This served to highlight how harsh the new regime was on the victims of industrial recession in communities which could offer no alternative source of employment. 'Under the operation of the New Poor Law', Richard Oastler, the factory reformer, wrote in 1841, 'England is reduced to a state of horrid barbarism'[8] – a judgement somewhat at odds with Margaret Thatcher's recent appraisal of 'Victorian values' and their merits.

Opposition was not confined to the social elite, but was manifest in the protests and riots that accompanied the implementation of the act all round the country. In the south, protest was isolated and sporadic; assaults on the new guardians and attacks on the work-houses were contained without undue difficulty in 1835–6. Even so, outbreaks of rural incendiarism in East Anglia at this time were provoked by the withdrawal of customary forms of support as well as the changes in the rural economy which made such support all the more vital. In March 1844, the *News of the World* reported the trial of Gifford White, indicted for sending a threatening letter to a local farmer, Isaac Ilett who, true to the principles of the new regime, had refused to take on extra hands at a time of local hardship.

We are determined to set fire to the whole of this place if you do not set us to work. . . . What do you think the young men are to do if you don't set them to work? They must do something. The fact is, we cannot go any longer. We must commit robbery and everything that is contrary to your wish.

The sentence of the court was transportation. There is evidence that starvation became a problem in some areas, particularly among the elderly, who found their small stipend from the rates reduced or removed under the new system.

Relief in the workhouse was available for those who truly had no other resources. However, we must not underestimate popular hatred of these 'New Bastilles' as they became called, nor the degree of suffering the unemployed were prepared to go through rather than submit to the indignity of what amounted to voluntary imprisonment. 'They won't give us anything except we goes into the house,' commented an old farm labourer in 1850, 'and as long as I can arne a sixpence anyhows, they sharn't part me from my wife.'9 For workers all round the country, outdoor relief had been regarded as a right; its abolition was therefore a contravention of natural justice. An anonymous Welsh worker noted how the new poor law operated in the interest of the capitalist classes and to the detriment of the working man:

We know that the framers of the law of our land will not make any law to amend or ameliorate our condition. Loading heavier, that is the religion of wealth. Lower, lower with the condition of workmen and more labour and 'that's the rub'. And after the workman fails to work, to the Bastille with him to be plagued, to be separated from his wife and children and to be slowly starved with water porridge.10

In the north, opposition was more widespread and more co-ordinated. In parts of Yorkshire, the houses of guardians and poor law supporters were ransacked, workhouses were burned and troops called in to restore order. In the early 1840s there was a national movement in the making on both sides of the Pennines; the anti-poor law movement became involved with the Chartists, who committed themselves to the law's repeal. In northern towns, workers were fearful that the new poor law would be used to transfer workless rural labourers into the expanding industrial towns, where they would be used to force down wages and break trade union organization. In the late 1830s, the Poor Law Commission set up migration offices in Manchester and Leeds to co-ordinate the transfer of surplus labour from the south. It never came to very much; most southern paupers had neither the skills nor the aptitude to adapt to work in the industrial areas and the initiative was soon dropped. The general drift of workers from East Anglia in particular was obvious, but little of it was subsidized by the poor law.

In the midlands and the textile towns, opposition from workers and ratepayers alike delayed the construction of workhouses and led to modifications in the new regulations. In the 1840s, amendments were passed allowing relief to widows, orphans and deserted mothers (within limits): those groups whose relationship to the labour market was viewed as problematic. Another act allowed relief to the unemployed on the completion of a labour test – usually stone-breaking or oakum-picking (the manual decomposition of old rope to obtain fibre for caulking) – outside the workhouse. And all round the country, various boards of guardians condoned the continuing relief of the elderly on the grounds of infirmity, for the sick were permitted to be relieved in their own homes. The drive for uniformity and the abolition of outdoor relief had failed to meet its objectives.

Such concessions and their implementation remained highly idiosyncratic. Research has shown how farmers in East Anglia, by notifying their unemployed workers as 'sick', continued to manage the local market much as they had always done. In Manchester, by contrast, a well-regulated workhouse epitomized the administration of the new poor law much as its creators had intended. In general, it became increasingly difficult for able-bodied unemployed men to get any help at all from the poor law during the nineteenth century, without submitting to hours of hard labour in the stoneyard or the indignities of the casual ward, which operated a punitive regime specifically designed to deter vagrancy. In 1870, the system was made even more restrictive, abolishing out-relief for the old and for large numbers of women on the grounds that many such paupers were still economically active and their stipend from the rates served to depress wages in the jobs they pursued, thereby extending pauperism and damaging the incentive to self-sufficiency. As late as the 1890s, the authorities were still agonizing about the ways in which easy access to poor relief increased the numbers dependent on public funds. Yet, at this time, both Seebohm Rowntree's study of York and Charles Booth's investigation in London showed that between a third and a half of working-class households had insufficient income to meet the absolute basic necessities of life. Public administrators, then as now, credited the poor with far more control over their working lives than was either realistic or feasible.

In the last decades of the century, both local authorities and charitable enterprise had moved into the vacuum left by the official system of poor relief in providing help for the unemployed. Such activities were prompted by the consequences of the Lancashire cotton famine in the 1860s and became more common as cyclical depressions hit Britain in the late 1870s, the 1880s and again in the mid-1890s. In industrial centres and major conurbations, various charities co-operated with local authorities on committees working to relieve the 'exceptional distress' caused by the depression in trade. By and large, these bodies aimed to separate the 'genuine' unemployed – the regular workman who had fallen temporarily on hard times – from the rest of the casual residuum, contaminated by drink, mendacity and chronic pauperism. The main exception to this trend was to be found in the work of the Salvation Army, created in the 1880s in the capital by William Booth. This organization sought the salvation of souls through the provision of work for the homeless and jobless and were not particularly choosey about who they took on. The Charity Organization Society, by contrast, was more selective and referred clients with a past history of drink, debt or irregular working habits to the tender mercies of the poor law.

The increase in the incidence of pauperism, coupled with the growth in the number of indoor paupers (the cost of maintaining an individual pauper rose by 100 per cent between 1870 and 1905), pushed the poor law in inner city areas into a state of total collapse. Plagued by the incessant demands of the chronic casuals and quite unable to raise sufficient rate money to meet their obligations, guardians in major conurbations were becoming increasingly reliant on loans from the Exchequer – loans which they had no hope of repaying. And by the turn of the century, Labour guardians were being elected whose ambitions were out of sympathy with financial probity and deterrent systems of relief and who had little intention of reducing debts at the cost of the poor. Neither did voluntary action reach the root of the problem. In 1885, the lord mayor of London launched the first in a series of annual appeals to raise funds to relieve the unemployed. In 1886, the President of the Local Government Board issued a circular to all local authorities encouraging them to do what many had already been doing, namely fund public works which would create jobs. The dimensions of the crisis no longer permitted a local solution.

Unemployment and the working class

The new poor law had made its mark on the attitudes of working people towards public relief. Well before 1834, it is clear that artisans and journeymen were reluctant to go cap-in-hand to the parish. However, the economic dislocations that accompanied the industrial revolution had made parish relief the last resort of a larger section of the working population than it had ever been before. Hence the demonstrations and riots that greeted the introduction of the new poor law were not the work of paupers alone, but of labourers and workers who realized that they were liable to resort to poor relief at some point in their lives. Once the initial opposition had been overcome, however, the system of deterrence worked only too well. No respectable worker – or his family – would turn to the poor law in time of distress. By the middle of the century, the name 'pauper' carried a social stigma second only to that of the convicted criminal.

Most workers went to inordinate lengths to avoid recourse to the relieving officer. In the mid–nineteenth century, we witness the huge expansion of clubs, societies and associations dedicated to the collection of contributions from working people in order to help them cope in the event of a crisis. For the most part, these concerned themselves with the loss of income due to sickness and the need to insure against the disgrace of a pauper funeral. Insurance against unemployment *per se* was less common. It was largely confined to skilled men in printing, construction, engineering, metal-working, shipbuilding and some of the older crafts in leather-working, bookbinding and furniture-making; it operated through the trade unions and was principally designed to prevent union men being forced to work below the recognized rate when desperate for want of work. In other sectors of the economy, notably mining and textiles, unions negotiated work-sharing systems as an alternative form of protection against the threat of recession. In this way, the negotiation of working practices was designed to protect jobs as well as maintain wages.

Unions which did provide help for those out of work, covering around 1 million members by 1906, did not distinguish very clearly between those idle due to dispute and those unemployed because of a depression in trade. In their eyes, members sacked by an employer for protecting trade practices were more entitled to help than the 'ordinary' unemployed. Because mutual insurance was officially encouraged, early trade unions tended to register as friendly societies in order to avoid the sanctions imposed on trade combinations in the early nineteenth century. Indeed, the decision to give full recognition to trade unions as such, taken in 1867, was largely due to their work as benefit societies. However, while official opinion encouraged some forms of self-help – like the provision of unemployment benefits – it frowned on others, like collective action to raise wages. When considering a national scheme of unemployment insurance early in the twentieth century, the government was also seeking to shape the provision of union benefits in a manner more in keeping with official ideas about who deserved the privilege of such support.

For the vast majority of the industrial workforce there was no automatic support to fall back on when recession struck. Only the most desperate swallowed their pride and sought help from the poor law or charity. The majority tried to maintain their self-esteem in much the same way as many unemployed families do today, by resorting to credit, to loan sharks or kindly relatives and neighbours on the understanding that debts would be repaid when times were not so hard. Then, the unemployment of the husband frequently pushed the wife into taking on more washing, more cleaning, child-minding, sewing, in order to supplement dwindling family resources. The local pawnshop was a familiar resort of many who carefully preserved a Sunday suit, a pair of decent shoes, a small piece of jewellery which could be pledged on the Monday and redeemed on the Friday when (and if) the wages arrived. In this fashion, working-class households survived on a precarious structure of credit that tended to collapse when employment was scarce, debts mounted, the rent was unpaid and creditors were at the door. By various systems and strategies, the families of unskilled labourers 'got by' most of the time, but without any security outside the informal help that might be forthcoming from family or friends.

The other resort of the unemployed was migration . . . from depressed to prosperous areas within the country, or emigration overseas to the colonies, where labour was still scarce. Many trade unions subsidized unemployed members who were prepared to 'tramp' in search of work. Although such mobility was less common among engineers and metal workers by the end of the century, skilled construction workers could only expect to receive help from their union if they moved around looking for a job. Some unions provided emigration for members willing to try their luck in the United States, Canada, even Australia; the Amalgamated Society of Engineers had branches in the colonies as early as the 1860s.

Although emigration remained an option for the young and skilled, the colonies could not be used as a dumping ground for Britain's surplus labour. Colonial governments in the 'white dominions' had no desire to act as the repository for British paupers any more than for British convicts. Moreover, the poorest guardians could not afford to pay the fares. By the turn of the century, some emigration schemes were still operating, but under the aegis of charity – not the poor law. The vast majority of the charity-assisted migrants were children, orphaned or abandoned, so the organizers claimed, and carefully vetted by the overseas authorities to eliminate unhealthy, criminal or otherwise undesirable elements. Those unemployed who made it overseas did so under their own steam or were recruited by agents looking for labour for the colonies in Britain, who offered assisted passages.

By the late nineteenth century, the appearance of large conurbations concentrated unemployment and underemployment in an unprecedented fashion. With the migration of the 'respectable' middle classes to the suburbs, those unable to earn a regular income were left behind, forming the backbone of an 'inner city' problem. It is unlikely that the temporarily unemployed labourer was really much worse off than his father or his grandfather had been. Rural underemployment had been much less visible than its urban counterpart; the proportion of the population that lived in towns and cities had expanded enormously since the days of the Chartists. The new visibility of labour market disorganization at home (while American and German industry were encroaching on British markets overseas), the extension of the franchise to most working men in 1884, the growth of trade and labour organization and the inability of traditional institutions to cope with the situation, all combined to promote the unemployment question as a key issue in national politics in the early twentieth century.

III

Theory and Opinion:
The Politics of Unemployment

Introduction

In the course of the nineteenth century, social enquiry fostered the development of more complex systems of social classification. Rather than being seen as a uniform, homogeneous whole, the construction of poverty began to be understood in terms of its apparent causes – and these were used to determine appropriate treatment. As a result, the classification of paupers became increasingly significant in determining the nature of public relief. The 'respectable' aged and infirm, for example, could be permitted extra privileges inside the workhouse – in the form of tobacco, beer and a better diet – while the itinerant casual vagrants were treated worse than most convicted criminals. Under the regulations laid down by the poor laws, the terms of relief offered to the able-bodied male pauper came nearer the latter category than the former. Indeed, the reform of the poor laws in the early 1830s had been carried out primarily with this group in mind. Idle habits and profligate ways were to be deterred and self-sufficiency to be restored through the consistent pursuit of policies which punished applicants for public relief by forcing them to submit to the workhouse and what amounted to voluntary imprisonment.

The strategy worked – after a fashion. In the course of the century, the numbers of men applying to the parish whose destitution could be ascribed to a 'want to employment' dwindled. The whole sphere of poor relief became viewed with loathing by the respectable working class. This revulsion has proved very long-lived. Its legacy is still visible in popular attitudes to means-tested public relief and to the extraction of compulsory task work in exchange for it. This goes some way towards explaining the current unpopularity of workfare.

By the end of the century, however, the utility of a uniform, deterrent system of relief was being drawn into question; new techniques for diagnosing and treating the causes of poverty were being developed. The emphasis was shifting away from the individual and his or her personal deficiencies and towards an understanding of structural and environmental factors that produced destitution. In short, many were poor for no fault of their own and to submit such cases to punitive treatment would not get anyone anywhere. The sick, for instance, were not going to recover more quickly by being forced to continue their search for work. On the contrary, further labour was liable to delay rather than promote recovery, and the resulting reduction in efficiency on the worker's part was hardly going to contribute to the prosperity of the industry he served. In the quarter century preceding the First World War, debates on the classification of social dependency began to acknowledge the existence of groups deserving of public support outside the purview of the poor law. Foremost among these were the aged poor and the unemployed.

From the introduction of this new category, it was clear that the label 'unemployed' did not apply to just anyone who claimed to be unable to find work. Privileged treatment was not to be accorded to those whose predicament could be attributed to such personal fault as idleness, fecklessness or poor working habits. In this country at least, the identification of the unemployed has never depended on the opinion of the client group itself. Unemployment in Britain has always been defined in terms of administrative processes, based on legislation deciding the rights of the jobless to social support. What was the 'pauper host' is now a multiplicity of different groups: 'pensioners', 'disabled', 'mentally handicapped', 'vagrants' and 'unemployed'. How these labels are determined and applied is neither clear nor simple, but is the result of a complex interaction of social conventions interpreted through political discussions and compromises that also change over time. At the end of the last century, attempts to draw up uniform criteria which would enable the 'unemployed' to be segregated from others without work were constantly frustrated by variations in local custom and practice, heterogeneous methods of labour management between different industries and the way these became reflected in different political assumptions and attitudes. It was one thing to acknowledge unemployment as a cause of destitution and quite another to give this understanding a practical application. Although we commonly interpret unemployment as an economic variable, in a very real sense it was – and is – a socially and politically constructed one.

Debate over unemployment and the identification of the unemployed was initially provoked by the series of cyclical booms and slumps which hit the British economy in the 1870s and 1880s. These provoked a rising incidence of public protest among those thrown out of work as a result, notably in major urban centres in the latter decade. The growth of major conurbations increased the dependence of the working population on the cash economy – and therefore paid employment – while simultaneously concentrating social distress and rendering it more visible. In the inner cities, agencies designed to cope with destitution were proving unequal to the strain; even philanthropic organizations were beginning to argue the case for increased state support. Although it took a quarter of a century to convert emergency intervention into permanent government policy, the framework for the debate was set in this period. This framework has continued to shape discussion both on the nature of the problem and the means of its solution ever since.

Unemployment: the early debate

In the closing years of the nineteenth century, unemployment became established as an issue of national importance. New social enquiry supported the notion of a 'deserving' unemployed. In his investigation of London's overstocked labour market in the late 1880s, Charles Booth went to some lengths to distinguish those whose poverty was ostensibly attributable to their own weaknesses – idleness, criminal disposition, profligacy, drunkenness or physical incapacity – from regular labourers wishing to gain full-time employment but unable to find it. Once the existence of a 'deserving unemployed' was acknowledged, it became increasingly obvious that a punitive poor law was inappropriate for dealing with them.

What incentive was there, after all, for workers to be sober, industrious and thrifty if, when recession struck, they received exactly the same treatment as those whose unemployment was apparently attributable to their personal faults? A proportion of these respectable unemployed were, moreover, skilled men whose services would again be required when trade recovered. Forcing them into the stoneyards was pointless; it would undermine their labour market status (thereby damaging their chances of re-entering full-time work) and it could impede the recovery of the industry to which they belonged.

The only permanent agencies which distinguished the 'deserving' and 'undeserving' cases were the trade unions. In the late nineteenth century, industrial organization was overwhelmingly concentrated among skilled workers. Moreover, unions differed considerably from their present-day counterparts in the way they offered broader forms of protection against a greater range of industrial and social risks. Many unions gave benefits to members who were sick or unemployed, in order to prevent them being forced, through poverty, to work for less than the union rate. In this way, welfare benefits were tied up with the protection of trade practices and negotiated rates of pay. Of course, not all unions could afford to offer such help and the great majority of the workforce belonged to no union at all. However, then as now, all were involved in protecting their members from the threat of redundancy: through negotiations on manning levels, hours of work, overtime, job demarcation and other industrial agreements – notably the use of short-time working in periods of recession.

The first official unemployment figures, published annually by the Board of Trade from 1886, were drawn from returns made by unions who provided these benefits. Quite obviously these data cannot provide an accurate guide to the overall numbers without jobs in this period; the experience of the skilled man was quite different from that of his unskilled counterpart and even further removed from the working life of the casual labourer. Over and above this, however, the nature of the 'unemployment' which entitled a member to union support was substantially different from our understanding of the term today. Many union men (and they were overwhelmingly men) lost work due to their defence of trade practices; members were expected to quit if their employer was in breach of trade agreements and would receive branch support for so doing. Similarly, an unemployed member would be expected to refuse 'black' work or a job in a 'blacked' shop for much the same reasons. Finally, the union member 'on the books' was not necessarily totally out of work. In skilled sectors of the construction industry, for example, members were obliged to tramp in search of work but were expected to pick up the odd casual job to supplement their benefit, on the understanding that it was not work 'in the trade'. The ironfounders operated a crude form of means testing, which determined how much an unemployed member was permitted to earn – again outside the trade – before he sacrificed his right to benefit.

Stepping back from the administrative detail, we can see that both the nature of unemployment and the identification of the unemployed were heavily bound up with trade practices and the bargaining procedures of specific industrial sectors. The 'unemployed' were hardly a uniform group, however much official statistics suggested otherwise. Nonetheless, union schemes offering unemployment benefits were well regarded in official circles because they protected the skilled regular workman from being forced to resort to the poor laws. And the methods adopted by skilled unions in construction, engineering, shipbuilding and the metal trades came to exert a marked influence on the formation of the world's first compulsory unemployment insurance scheme, introduced by the Liberal government in 1911.

The expansion of such forms of mutual self-help encountered formidable obstacles: the inability of even regular general labourers to afford the subscriptions (union dues were high in skilled sectors), opposition among employers to union organization and – most pertinently – the impact of recurring slumps on the viability of union finances in the years preceding the First World War. Following the major depression of the mid-1880s, the old alliance between labour and the Liberal Party began to show signs of strain. Mass unemployment fostered the spread of socialist ideologies among the working class; in London, the Social Democratic Federation (SDF) – a revolutionary Marxist society – organized mass demonstrations among the unemployed themselves, bringing their plight more directly to the attention of the authorities. In the industrial north, notably Scotland, the Independent Labour Party began to return its own MPs, who demanded a far greater degree of intervention from Westminister than was tolerable to a Liberal Party still dominated by Gladstonian ideals of *laisser faire*. The extension of public works and the statutory shortening of the working day to eight hours won support not only from the ILP and the SDF but also from the TUC, which also favoured the introduction of immigration controls to reduce the competition for work. Originally, the industrial labour movement had favoured using collective bargaining to shorten the working day but, by the early 1890s, the difficulty of securing concessions from increasingly recalcitrant employers and the grow-ing unionization of unskilled workers, where weaker organization rendered industrial pressure less effective, were both pushing the TUC in the direction of promoting a legislative solution to the unemployment problem.

Alleviating the effects of unemployment by shortening the working day was hardly a novel solution, even in the 1880s when the Eight Hour League was established to secure that end. In the 1840s, Engels had noted how, when times were hard, employers in certain industries tended to discharge hands while lengthening the hours of work for those who were left:

> If a manufacturer can employ ten hands nine hours daily, he can employ nine if each works ten hours and the tenth goes hungry. And if a manufacturer can force the nine hands to work an extra hour daily for the same wages by threatening to discharge them at a time when the demand for hands is not very great, he discharges the tenth and saves so much wages. This is the process on a small scale, which goes on in a nation in a large one.[1]

The object of many labour demands both at that time and since was to put the process into reverse: to shorten the working day in periods of recession, thereby sharing work and preventing redun-dancy . . . and preferably without a proportional reduction in wages. The Eight Hour League argued that literally hundreds of thousands of jobs could be created in this fashion. The movement peaked in the early 1890s; in the 1892 general election, support for legislation to reduce the working day became essential for Liberal candidates in many areas, if they wished to secure working-class votes. In response to the demands of the Amalgamated Society of Engineers (ASE, forerunner of the present day AUEW) a number of employers did agree to reduce working hours in the early 1890s, including the Woolwich Arsenal. The results were not encouraging. When hours were shortened, productivity rose; there was therefore no corresponding rise in the demand for labour to maintain output. As a result, support for this particular solution dwindled and the labour movement put increasing emphasis on state-sponsored jobs as the means of securing the 'right to work'. By the turn of the century, organized labour was presenting a fairly cogent set of policies, demanding that central government take charge of the unemployment problem by providing jobs on demand at union rates for all who needed them.

Such policies required a complete revolution in the role of the state in labour market management and embodied a far more generous view of how the 'unemployed' should be identified than that found in official circles. Basically, for the left, the 'unemployed' were those looking for work who were physically capable of performing it. The policy of public works at a fair wage was complemented by demands for universal free education, state pensions for the elderly and more help for the sick, widows and orphans outside the embrace of the poor laws. The notion of a 'residuum' was not eliminated altogether. It tended to be confined to the unrespectable unskilled – blacklegs, petty criminals, drunkards – who remained outside the labour movement. As union membership expanded, so this element shrank in size. In the absence of state intervention, trade unions – true to the precepts embodied in the Eight Hours League – tried to protect the rank and file by spreading work as far as possible while keeping wage rates as high as possible, with varying degrees of success. Such strategies did little to rationalize the use of labour (but then there was no reason for labour to co-operate in promoting the interests of capital); they did, however, offer a modicum of protection from poverty and the exigencies of the poor laws.

Theoretical justification for extending the role of the state varied considerably. The leadership of the SDF saw it as the natural consequence of the revolutionary overthrow of industrial capitalism, which, initially at least, would require the state to take over the running of a new economy based on socialist principles. Such aspirations remained confined to a minority; most on the left looked to more gradualist methods of promoting an equitable society through the combined means of industrial bargaining and parliamentary reform. Support for a higher degree of state regulation was most cogently and coherently expressed by the leaders of the Fabian Society, Sydney and Beatrice Webb.

The Fabians in general, the Webbs in particular, were ardent believers in central planning and state control as the means to raise national efficiency and eventually, through legislative reform, to achieve socialism. 'Socialism', in their book, was less to do with mass participation in political decision-making than with the promotion of a more rational society through the centralization of authority in the hands of an impartial, professional bureaucracy. In this respect, Fabian ideology can be contrasted both with nineteenth-century *laisser faire* and with late twentieth-century economic theories, which have revived faith in market mechanisms and free competition as the means to promote the general good. For the Fabians, however, the disorganization of urban labour markets and the physical and mental degeneration they fostered demonstrated the inefficiencies inherent in such a system. The poor laws may have reduced the costs of maintaining the poor, but they had not attacked the root causes of poverty, which were undermining the future prosperity of the nation. In short, the poor laws had to go. Reform was to be achieved by the application of scientific principle at central level. Government departments, operating through specialized local agencies, would be able to identify, analyse and eliminate the various causes of social distress.

As far as the labour market was concerned, the rationalization of employment practices was essential and to be achieved through the compulsory registration of all job vacancies and unemployed at state-run labour bureaux, where officials would match vacancies and unemployed labour with minimal delay. Those deemed physically unfit would be removed from the labour market; those disinclined to work regularly would be retained in labour colonies and workers immediately surplus to requirements would be employed in state–run municipal workshops. In times of chronic distress, the government would set in motion programmes of contra–cyclical public works, the cost of which would be recovered through taxation once recovery was secured. Finally, to improve Britain's industrial performance, the state was to play a far greater role in the education and training of the future workforce. Sydney Webb in particular was a strong advocate of extensive state intervention in this area, to allow working–class children to achieve their full potential, be this of an intellectual or technical nature. In the view of the Webbs, unemployment was one manifestation of the inefficiency of the market when left to its own devices, an inefficiency that could be removed with the correct application of scientific principles and state planning.

The Fabians joined the ILP, the TUC and other socialist societies to form the Labour Representation Committee in 1900, which was the ancestor of the Labour Party. In some ways, it was an unfortunate alliance. Fabian ideas about how a socialist state might be achieved were severely at odds with those manifest elsewhere on the left. Labour market reforms proposed by the Webbs and their allies vested authority in central bodies of professionals and experts, not in collective bargaining, still less in local democracy. Fabian views on the extension of official controls over issues such as training and employment were somewhat at odds with existing apprenticeship systems and closed shop agreements that under-pinned the bargaining position of many skilled unions. Beatrice Webb made little secret of her distaste for trade unionism in general – or of her dislike of many union leaders whose views she found bigoted and whose methods were distinctly at odds with her own notions of national efficiency. Nonetheless, the Fabians were influential. They formed the nub of the Progressive Alliance which ran the London County Council at the turn of the century; this introduced one of the first systems of labour registries which sent the unemployed to publicly funded work on road and building maintenance and in the capital's parks. Through such experiments, their knowledge of the labour market, their political and social contacts, the Webbs came to exert influence in policy-making circles.

The Fabian Society was not isolated in its enthusiasm for labour market reform which, at this time, was widely linked to questions of industrial performance and national efficiency. The problem of social distress came to attract the attention of a new generation of social scientists. The challenge posed to Britain's position in world markets by newly industrialized countries – notably Germany and the United States – was met by efforts to raise productivity through the introduction of new technology and tighter supervision of the production process. In this context, questions of manpower management became central, the pace of work increased and the rejection of those unable to keep up added further to the unemployment problem. Social enquiry revealed that labour markets in major conurbations did not present an encouraging picture. Far from operating at maximum efficiency, they showed every sign of being overcrowded, disorganized and corrupt. Work was not necessarily allocated to the most competent applicant, but to the known face, the man prepared to bribe for the privilege, the most desperate candidate, who would accept a lower wage but might be incapable of doing a decent job. In major commercial centres, where irregular employment was widespread, pauperism was endemic. Chronic poverty and poor environment fostered physical disabilities; the shortcomings of the local labour force encouraged employers to import rural workers, thereby adding to the oversupply found in inner cities and making the competition for work at the bottom end of the market fiercer than ever. Theories abounded concering the progressive degeneration of the urban workforce and the imminent collapse of both economy and Empire. To correct these abuses and to encourage the labour market to operate in the manner free market economists suggested it should, a modicum of state regulation and rationalization began to appear an attractive solution. To paraphrase a prominent supporter of British capitalism and the Empire, Lord Milner, reform was not simply a matter of philanthropy, it was vital for business.

Not all observers, however, agreed that the state should intervene in this fashion. Traditions of *laisser faire* did not evaporate overnight and, in many circles, official intervention was still viewed as counterproductive. State regulation would raise industrial costs, thus further damaging Britain's competitive edge in overseas markets, as well as diverting funds available for investment to unprofitable ends. Such attitudes characterized the Liberal Party in the years of Gladstone's leadership. Not surprisingly, they remained strong among poor law officials, who continued to stress that the personal inadequacies of the underemployed casuals were responsible for their plight, disregarding broader economic and structural factors which influenced the competition for jobs. Because many unemployed shied away from entering the workhouse and refused to labour in the poor law stoneyards, their predicament could not be genuine, but the result of innate idleness. Lax administration of relief to such people only encouraged their vices and caused the numbers of so-called unemployed to rise in direct proportion to the amount of help available to them. The provision of state benefits on a generous scale therefore appeared to expand the very client group whose plight they were designed to ameliorate. Applicants only resorted to official agencies as an easier option to unpleasant or unconducive work. Their unemployment was therefore voluntary. Here we find the notion of 'benefit induced' unemployment, so prominent among monetarist economists in the 1970s, in its nineteenth-century form. Then as now, the solution to the problem was assumed to lie in the tighter administration of official help and minimal state intervention in order to restore personal initiative and self-reliance and to minimize the burden on the economy, while encouraging charitable organizations to cater for any unfortunate anomalies that might arise.

Even those who advocated reform did not always argue that state intervention was the best way to achieve it. One of the most influential pioneers of labour market investigation and reform, Charles Booth, promoted the rationalization of labour supply and demand in casual labour markets, while resisting the notion of extensive state regulation to achieve these ends. Basing his analysis of the labour market's ills on an extensive survey of East London, including an unprecedented classification of the 'residuum', Booth favoured decasualization as the key remedy to the unemployment problem. This would allow the more easy distinction between those who would not work regularly, those who could not, and the casuals who would seize the chance of a permanent job if the opportunity arose. The proliferation of short-term engagements raised the cost of labour to employers while simultaneously exacerbating underemployment and poverty in the workforce. The spread of trade unionism had done little to help. 'It has been the usual policy of trade unions to raise the rate of pay and shorten the tenure of employment,' Booth argued to an Official Select Committee investigating the issue in 1893. 'This policy of short tenure for high wages tends to increase the numbers required to do a certain amount of work, while at the same time it tends to decrease the amount of work available'. The answer lay in the removal of inefficient and inferior workers, allowing the rest to enjoy regular earnings at more realistic rates of pay. Initially, Booth wished to extend the powers of the state in their traditional punitive mode, to run corrective 'labour colonies' to rehabilitate this element of the 'residuum'. Those who failed to respond to a regime of state-contracted work under close supervision would be consigned to the poorhouse or the prison.

Booth did not concentrate only on the reduction of labour supply, he also sought – in his later work – to remedy defects in demand. The removal of the incompetent and the idle was best undertaken, not by state agencies, but by employers themselves, either singly or in combination; this would allow them to rationalize labour management and reduce their costs. Under such circumstances, the labour market itself would act to abstract the most expendable casuals, a process which would provide the necessary discipline to encourage the incorrigible wastrel to mend his ways. However, it was obvious that not all casuals were capable of working full-time and nor could they all respond to the peculiar stimulus provided by the poor law. Hence Booth became something of a reluctant convert to the merits of state pensions to allow the elderly, incapacitated worker to quit the labour market altogether. For Booth, the object of the exercise was to make the labour market work better; he was far less concerned with rehabilitating its victims.

Booth made some effort to promote his decasualization programme on the docks in both London and Liverpool, but with no marked success. However popular his ideas among his fellows in the Royal Statistical Society, he found fewer supporters within industry itself and, for reforms that depended on voluntary incentive, this antagonism proved fatal. Labour leaders understandably argued that his system of extending the sphere of permanent employment would reduce the chances of work for most of their members while tightening managerial discipline over the rest. Port employers, on the other hand, did not agree that casualism was expensive and inefficient, claiming that insecurity of employment and the prospect of bonus payments for fast work extracted greater effort from the workers. As a result, voluntary decasualization proved to be singularly ineffective and those who sympathized with Booth's ideas became ever more convinced of the need for state action to secure reform.

By the early twentieth century, informed opinion was generally far more supportive of state intervention than it had been a decade earlier. The debacle of the Boer War and the subsequent revelations about the state of working-class health, the growing influence of Labour in local government and poor law administration, the continuing effects of the trade cycle all prompted both Liberals and Conservatives to take a renewed interest in the question of unemployment. Now the aim was to establish a state policy on a permanent basis. The provision of emergency schemes of public works, hitherto the main focus of both public and charitable agencies, had always been undertaken as temporary measures, designed to tide over the 'deserving' unemployed until prosperity returned. Experience had revealed the shortcomings of such a strategy. The desired clientele rarely came forward and the schemes were swamped with applications from casuals who viewed them as another source of temporary work in hard times – and who returned to them in the winter months with a depressing regularity. The Conservatives tended to see the problem as one of scale. Under the promptings of Joseph Chamberlain, they came out in favour of introducing a tariff on imported goods. This would both protect jobs at home and raise the money necessary to fund more extensive public works. Although support for free trade was still strong enough to secure the return of the Liberal Party with a large majority in the general election of 1906, rising levels of unemployment in the ensuing years forced the new government to search for an alternative solution. This was found in the work of the young William Beveridge, introduced by Beatrice Webb to Winston Churchill, the newly appointed and highly ambitious President of the Board of Trade in the Asquith administration.

Like Booth, William Beveridge was a student of the London labour market, and used this to generalize both about the ills of the labour market as a whole and the policies that might be introduced to cure them. *Unemployment, a Problem of Industry* was first published in 1909. Its findings differed remarkably little from Booth's of twenty years earlier; both promoted decasualization as the means to draw a firmer line between efficient and inefficient labour. Unlike Booth, however, Beveridge showed no interest in the correction of individual working habits, but sought to reform labour market practices by making it impossible for the casual labourer to work in an irregular fashion. Unlike Booth again, Beveridge was a firm believer in state action. At the same time, his faith in collectivism was far more circumscribed than that of the Webbs; state intervention was designed to promote the smooth operation of the free market, not to replace it. The object was to eliminate the waste of labour as a national resource, a waste which both undermined industrial efficiency and rendered sobriety, hard work and good character of little account in the allocation of jobs. For Beveridge, the introduction of the tariff served no purpose. It subjected the economy to an unnecessary degree of regulation and, by pouring money into public works, fostered casualism when the object of policy should be to eradicate it. The only viable unemployment policy had to focus on the rationalization of hiring procedures, to separate the unemployed from the unemployable and to allow state help to reach the former. The means proposed to achieve these ends were a centrally regulated system of labour exchanges and a national scheme of compulsory unemployment insurance.

Labour exchanges would act to co-ordinate labour supply with available vacancies. Public officials would be in a position to distinguish between the idler and the genuine workman and would allocate jobs in such a fashion as to prevent the former getting any work at all. Beveridge declared to the Royal Commission on the Poor Laws in 1907: 'For the man who wants to get a casual job now and again, the exchange will make that wish impossible . . . The result of the exchange is the direct opposite from that of assisting the lazy or incapable; it makes it harder for them and compels them to be regular.'[2] At the same time, Beveridge saw that the root of the problem of underemployment stemmed from the demand by employers for casual labour. Working in co-operation with Llewel-lyn Smith, prominent social statistician and head of the Labour Department, he helped introduce subtle financial inducements into the 1911 National Insurance Act – so subtle that they passed unremarked by nearly all employers – to encourage the rationaliza-tion of employment by charging higher contributions to those using casual workers. In the event, these incentives had very little effect; once again, entrenched industrial practices proved resistant to voluntary incentives to change.

However, in the introduction of unemployment insurance, we can observe how the 'morality of mathematics', as Churchill called it, served to divide the unemployed sheep from the unemployable goats. The 'unemployed' were defined as those normally in regular employment (with a record of contributions to prove it) who suffered short, temporary spells without work, because of fluctua-tions in trade, seasonal adjustments, or similar circumstances strictly beyond the individual's control. The limit set on the number of benefit weeks available, together with the need to prove six days' continuous unemployment before a claim would be met, aimed to prevent casuals being classed as 'unemployed'. The object of the exercise was to promote the efficient use of manpower resources by segregating the workforce into those with regular employment and those with none. The former would be recognized as 'unemployed' when temporarily out of work: the latter were not 'unemployed' at all, but formed part of the residuum of inefficient workers surplus to industrial requirements. If elderly, they could claim the newly introduced state pension; if ill, they could claim health benefit under the health insurance scheme. If their idleness could not be attributed to either of these, then it must be caused by failure of character and the punitive poor law was the appropriate agency for them. It is no coincidence that access to outdoor relief by the able-bodied was tightened up in the same year that unemployment benefits were first introduced.

In this manner, the respectable worker was saved from contami-nation through contact with the rest of the pauper class, as he was allowed benefit 'as of right' if ill or out of work. Prevailing working practices found in shipbuilding, construction, engineering, metal-working (the trades covered by this first unemployment scheme) provided the framework for a normative identity of 'the unemployed' which Beveridge and his colleagues tried unsuccessfully to superimpose on less organized labour markets. These norms have proved extraordinarily powerful and still underpin our understanding of 'unemployment' today. They were largely developed from the unemployment schemes operated by skilled unions in these sectors, stripped of any association with union organization or the protection of trade practices (those who lost work through disagreements over pay or working conditions were excluded). The new system of classification did not recognize 'long term' unemployment: the legal definition of 'unemployment' did not permit its existence – which is quite a different matter from saying that it did not occur. Nor did the 1911 act offer anything to trades in which the consequences of recession were met by work-sharing systems of some kind (split-shift or short-time) rather than by wholesale redundancies. This did not matter too much as long as state insurance was confined to trades where such practices were not prevalent. However, the wholesale extension of this new legislative formula to most branches of manual labour after the war superimposed a uniform definition of unemployment on diverse industrial practices in an unrealistic fashion. Whether Beveridge himself intended to design different forms of insurance to suit particular industries is a moot point. In his evidence to a Royal Commission investigating a bankrupt unemployment insurance scheme in the early 1930s, he claimed to have always been an advocate of such structural flexibility, although there is little sign of this in his early work.

The importance of this debate on the foundations of unemployment policy lies in the way it established unemployment as a single, uniform construct, stripped of its earlier associations with industrial bargaining. To some extent, the development of an homegeneous term to describe diverse consequences of industrial recession was the result of the policy-making process itself. Power was concentrated in the hands of professional social scientists to a quite exceptional extent. The nature of the problem was largely approached through the medium of statistics, which gave diverse experiences the appearance of uniformity. Hence the issue of casualism – repeatedly the subject for social scientific analysis – dominated official thinking to the detriment of other aspects of the problem. No attention was given to the impact of trade depression on one-industry towns in the north, for example, whose victims were not helped by the new initiatives. Policy was imposed, from the top down, by men with no direct experience of industry, beyond their own observations, and still less intention of acquiring any by involving outsiders in policy formation. By its very nature, the involvement of industry would divert official policy from its supposed foundation on scientific impartiality. However, this meant that the discourse about the construction of unemployment and the identity of the 'real' unemployed had reached no permanent conclusion. In the aftermath of the First World War, a newly strengthened labour movement started forcing its own demands on to the political agenda in a way it had not been powerful enough to do before. In the interwar period, however, the issue became inextricably entangled with the question of state benefits and who had the right to claim them, matters which will be covered in the next chapter.

Conclusion

Under the guidance of Margaret Thatcher, the Conservative administrations of the 1980s have set out to promote 'Victorian values' as the basis for restoring a different relationship between state and society – one which fosters self-sufficiency, rewards initiative, encourages independence from a so-called 'nanny' state. As part of this process, state regulation of the labour market has been 'rolled back' in recent years: access to benefits has become harder and levels of state support lower in an attempt to push social dependents back into waged work. A restored faith in the merits of competition as the vital foundation for industrial and economic efficiency has justified increasing the involvement of the private sector in the provision of public services. Cleaning, catering and similar low level jobs in the health and in local authority services have been subcontracted to outside agencies, to cut costs and encourage competition. Similar developments have been observed affecting the employment practices of many private firms. While this has also been true of professional services, most of the workers involved at the lower end of the market are employed on a part-time basis on short-term contracts. What we are witnessing, in short, is the recasualization of employment – with the government's positive encouragement.

The reasons why employers choose to comply are not hard to find. Part-time workers – defined as those working less than twenty-seven hours each week – are not covered by national insurance, employment protection legislation, private pension schemes or the right to holidays with pay. Using them to replace full-time workers allows the employer to make substantial savings in terms of overhead costs. Over and above this, the government has introduced special schemes to encourage job-sharing and part-time working, both among its own employees and in the private sector. Of course, no one in part-time work, however meagre, counts as 'unemployed'. However, that is a side issue; the main point being that the official incentives Beveridge originally designed to promote decasualization have been turned around to foster the type of labour market their creator was most concerned to destroy.

How far a less-regulated labour market will prove capable of performing more efficiently is hard to predict. Historical evidence on this point is, to say the least, not very encouraging. It is worthwhile noting that, by the early twentieth century and after decades of open competition, the party of *laisser faire*, then the Liberals, was quite convinced of the need for state regulation to eliminate the market's worst excesses. The conviction did not spring from a partial conversion to watered down socialism or a wishy-washy desire to help the poor. Rather it was founded on the concern of politicians for the long-term future of the British economy. Tory and Liberal imperialists and Fabian coefficients were united in the view that allowing the labour market to flounder on in an unregulated fashion would undermine the viability of industry and national prosperity. There were good capitalist reasons for supporting reform. Britain's leaders only had to look across the Channel to observe how state intervention in the German labour market was producing a better-trained, less poverty-stricken work-force – and how German economic growth rates were booming as a result.

Liberal policies to eliminate the use of casual labour and to identify – and help – the 'deserving' unemployed were justified both by the results of the first major surveys into the problem of poverty and by the social theories concerning urban degeneration that, in part, developed from them. Social scientists showed then what similar surveys show now: that the problem of poverty was most acute for those reliant on low-waged or intermittent work, especially for those households where the chief wage-earner was female. In such conditions, poor amenities and a hand-to-mouth existence encouraged the oldest children to leave school to seek work at the first available opportunity, thereby, in the longer term, adding to the glut of inexperienced, unqualified general labourers. Too much competition for too little work meant no one got enough to live on. This tended to undermine both the physical and mental capacities of the worker; the desperate, the inefficient and the idle clogged up the labour market, damaging both the incentive of other labourers to work hard and steadily, as well as the efficiency of those industries reliant on casual workers.

Booth, Beveridge and other social observers were convinced that underemployment and an insecure working life bred unemployability. Men hardened to casualism were unable to hold down a full-time job. 'Some are utterly incapable of working for four continuous hours' an observer of the casual labour market recorded in 1911. 'Many can do a hard day's work, but fail to be regular or punctual at the end of a week or a month . . . The secret of a steady normal life is gone from them.'³ Such were the working habits that characterized the residuum of the labour force. The longer a man was subject to a casual regime, the less likely he would be able to adjust to regular employment. In this way, the labour market became subdivided into two distinct groups – and mobility between the two was strictly one way. It was because casualism was expanding and because the 'deserving' unemployed were forced to resort to casual trades to find work that social theorists argued in favour of reform to contain degeneration and to protect those whose skills were vital to the nation's future prosperity.

More recently, exponents of dual labour market theories have developed similar analytical frameworks when examining employment trends in the 1970s. In this case, the labour force is divided into a 'core' sector in full-time employment and the 'periphery' which is

[67]

used on a part-time, irregular basis, to cope with fluctuations in demand (the same basis on which casuals were used a century earlier). Again, the insecurity and irregularity of the peripheral worker renders him – or, more likely, her – totally unsuitable for permanent employment. Again, the labour market subdivides as a result; the regular worker is endowed with a regular income and all the social benefits found in recent welfare legislation (national insurance protection, company pension, security of employment and so on), while workers in the peripheral sector, who are more liable to suffer poverty, are left with nothing. In the late 1970s, dual labour market theory was adapted by social scientists of a marxist persuasion; it became viewed as a strategy of 'divide and rule', used by capitalism to undermine working-class solidarity, in a manner that would have horrified Beveridge. Such 'deviations' aside, the similarity between labour market theories divided in time by nearly a century indicates that both are describing similar phenomena. Of course, such judgements are relative, and obviously the vocabulary has changed, but we are still left with the unpleasant sensation that, in spite of the Conservative's claim to have introduced a revolution in policy, we are moving back to forms of employment reminiscent of a much earlier era.

IV

Redefining Unemployment: The Interwar Years

Introduction

In the autumn of 1920, the brief boom that followed the First World War collapsed. The numbers out of work trebled in six months to reach 2,171,000 by June the following year. This set the pattern for the rest of the interwar period; unemployment remained over 1 million until the run up to the Second World War. The heart of the problem lay with the export trades. In December 1922, insured unemployment in shipbuilding, for example, was 35.6 per cent; as a result, towns heavily dependent on the industry, like Barrow in Furness and Jarrow, suffered unemployment rates of nearly 50 per cent at a time when the national average was just over 12 per cent. This industry, together with coal-mining, cotton textiles, engineering and the metal trades, accounted for half of all unemployment in the 1920s. Hence unemployment was concentrated in those areas – Scotland, northern Britain, south Wales, northern Ireland – where the staple export industries were located. Nor did matters improve with the passage of time. The Wall Street Crash of 1929 radically reduced levels of world trade and made the plight of Britain's heavy industries even worse. The result was an ever-sharper geographical polarization of unemployment. In the midlands and south-east, manufacture of consumer products boomed in the mid-1930s behind the protection of tariff barriers. At the same time, long-term unemployment developed in the depressed areas where industrial stagnation seemed interminable.

It is worth noting how contemporary attitudes towards the unemployment problem changed during these years. Certainly the First World War itself was extremely important. The war emergency created chronic manpower shortages. The notoriously unemployable 'residuum' – beloved of so many social investigators during the Edwardian era – melted away as the demands of the trenches and the munitions factories absorbed an ever-growing proportion of the adult population. Thanks to full employment, the power of organized labour, at both the workplace and the ballot-box, grew enormously. This growth continued even after the war was over; in 1920, nearly 50 per cent of the workforce belonged to a trade union and collective bargaining was formally established in a wide range of industries where previously it had been unknown. The emergence of the labour movement as a major political force did more than anything else to change the whole framework within which unemployment policy was framed and discussed. It was no longer politically feasible to talk in terms of an impartial, 'scientific' solution to labour market problems. Furthermore, wartime management of manpower resources had thoroughly discredited central government as a viable agency for labour market reform in the eyes of industrialists and trade unionists alike. After the Armistice, both sides of industry sought to consolidate their respective positions in the management of industrial affairs and to limit future bureaucratic intervention in this area.

Central government had no intention of perpetuating wartime controls for peacetime purposes. On the contrary, interwar governments were only too ready to let industry take care of itself. Prevailing faith in the free market, a faith which had characterized Victorian Britain, reasserted itself after the war. The old team which had developed the framework for prewar unemployment policy was disbanded in 1916. Beveridge spent the remaining years of the war at the Ministry of Food; Llewellyn Smith became Chief Industrial Adviser at the Board of Trade. By 1919, the Treasury was beginning to consolidate its control over policy. In the 1920s – much like the 1980s – state regulation of market forces was broadly viewed as counterproductive. If the export trades were depressed, this was because they were uncompetitive. Markets could be regained only if costs were cut and this meant that wages had to be reduced if jobs were to be preserved. Then as now, attention was paid to the dangers of inflation (which severely disrupted the economies of Germany and central Europe in the years following the war) and to the importance of maintaining a stable and strong currency. Then as now, many on the political right argued that the blame for high unemployment lay with the trade unions. The coal disputes of 1926 and 1985 were, broadly, over the same issue: whether government should subsidize jobs and wages in an industry where production was outstripping demand. And in both cases, the government's side of the argument carried the day.

It is not possible, however, to understand public policy for the unemployed in the interwar years in terms of Westminister and Whitehall alone. Local government was still very important. Local authorities created public works to absorb unemployed labour. Local poor law guardians were still obliged to provide relief for those unemployed who were, for one reason or another, unable to claim unemployment benefit under the national scheme. Even after the abolition of the guardians in 1929, the administration of the interwar equivalent of income support remained in the hands of local officials, frequently the same people, whose change of title did not necessarily reflect any change in practice. The stigma attached to the poor law's test of destitution passed directly to the household means test of the 1930s. In spite of official protests to the contrary, the degradation of the claimant remained a thorn in the flesh of the long-term unemployed.

Certainly, in political terms, the influence of the labour movement on unemployment policy was much more marked at local than at national level at this time. The earliest activities of the National Unemployed Workers' Committee Movement (later called the National Unemployed Workers' Movement – NUWM) were directed at local councils and boards of guardians: to force them to raise scales of relief or to expand the scope of public works schemes. The arrival of universal manhood suffrage – and the removal of pauper disqualification – in 1918 made locally elected officials much more sensitive to popular demand than they had been before the war. In the early 1920s at least, Labour-dominated councils developed more extensive public works and Labour boards of guardians revolutionized the administration of poor relief. Such practices contrasted with the growing parsimony imposed by the Conservative government later in the decade. As in the 1980s, central control of local activity thus became a key political issue in this period.

Not that central government could ever wash its hands of the unemployment problem, however appealing such a solution was to the Treasury. The 1911 National Insurance Act had set an important precedent; it had acknowledged the right of some workers to state support when out of a job. As this was an insurance scheme, there was no way that any government could wind it up without being accused of evading its obligations to existing contributors. The intervention of war reinforced official obligations; returning war heroes could not be left to the tender mercies of the poor law if they failed to find work without provoking a national scandal. In the event, the operation of the national insurance scheme became the main arena for unemployment policy debates. This scheme was both the instrument used for defining the nature of the problem and the main form of state help for the unemployed.

Reconstructing unemployment 1914–1939

In the interwar years, unemployment policy focused principally on the issue of unemployment relief. The potential of public works, the mainstay of official policy in the late nineteenth century, was discredited. Ostensibly designed to help the regular worker who had fallen on hard times, such schemes had deteriorated to the point where they had become just one more source of temporary employment in the casual's perennial round. Although still favoured by Labour councils in the 1920s as a strategy for helping the unemployed, Whitehall tended to view public works as an expensive option – and one not to be encouraged in the prevailing financial climate. Official enquiry in 1931 revealed that casualism was being fostered and perpetuated by such initiatives. Moreover, it cost around £324 per annum to employ a man on public works, while it only cost £74 per annum to keep him on the dole. In an era characterized by financial probity, this factor alone was enough to ensure the demise of schemes to create work for those with none. As unemployment peaked in 1932, those that had survived – largely works financed by the Road Fund – went into abeyance. At their height, in 1930, they had employed 56,000 people; at the time unemployment stood at 2.5 million.

Official provision of unemployment benefit was hardly uncontroversial. In a very real sense, receipt of state benefit demarcated the 'unemployed' sheep from the herd of pauper goats. Because help was not stigmatized by any association with the poor law, and because it was available irrespective of any other resources the claimant might possess, most of the jobless fought hard to be included in this privileged category. Equally, because the overall costs of state benefits rose with the levels of unemployment, the Treasury pushed for the use of regulations to contain the numbers of successful claims. Political debate at this time is reminiscent of discussions in recent years. Again, high levels of benefit were deemed to prevent wages reaching a 'realistic' level and to foster malingering at public expense (thus promoting 'voluntary' unemployment, in more modern terms). Contributions to national insurance were a burden for British exports. In a broader context, we can see that such discussions were basically concerned with determining the 'real' dimensions of the problem. Those on the right tended to argue that too many claimants were in point of fact not unemployed but unemployable, while their opponents claimed that official policy should embrace all who sought work but were unable to find it. After the Armistice, the rising tide of industrial militancy and the return of a war-weary army both rendered old preconceptions about the limited definition of unemployment politically untenable.

The difficulty of maintaining the formula reached in 1911 became evident in the early years of the war. In 1916, the unemployment scheme provoked opposition among trade unionists. In that year, the government tried to extend contributory insurance to cover industries liable to suffer from recession when the war ended. The initiative failed because workers refused to co-operate. Union leaders in cotton textiles, boots and shoes and other industries argued that, under the state scheme, their members would be forced to pay contributions while, thanks to the use of short-time working in these sectors in times of slack trade, they would never have the chance to claim benefit. In more general terms, the labour movement disliked the contributory scheme. It forced workers to pay the cost of supporting the unemployed while the general taxpayer escaped virtually scot-free. Left to their own devices, unions in skilled trades could give better rates of benefit for lower premiums than those available under the national scheme. After 1920, however, mass unemployment undermined the viability of earlier forms of union support. Industrial labour united behind the slogan 'Work or Maintenance': unemployment was in no way the fault of the working class and support for the jobless should be a national charge.

Revolution in Russia and Europe at the time of the Armistice fostered fears in Cabinet that unrest at home might be a prelude to serious political instability. The best strategy – and one in keeping with Lloyd George's political aptitude – was to buy off trouble. Hence, the out of work donation, introduced at the end of the war for soldiers and civilians alike, provided unemployment benefits virtually on demand at roughly four times the prewar rate. This cost a prodigious amount and won itself the total animosity of the Treasury. The scheme lasted two years and set something of a precedent for the future. It was brought to a close as the postwar boom collapsed. Unemployment rocketed in the winter of 1920–1 and the bill to extend the contributory system established in 1911, introduced the previous autumn, was rendered inoperable before it was ever implemented. As unemployment continued to rise, marches and demonstrations all round the country demanded the right to work or decent levels of state support. As ex-servicemen formed a sizeable component of the unemployed, the Lloyd George coalition prudently revised its ideas about how the problem should be tackled in order to forestall further unrest.

As a result, prewar unemployment policy was turned on its head. Far from trying to tidy up employment and decasualize the workforce, the Cabinet now positively encouraged work-sharing in order to spread such work as was available as widely as possible. In 1922, the government allowed short-time workers to claim unemployment benefit to supplement reduced earnings, a decision that must have set Edwin Chadwick spinning in his grave. At the same time, access to benefits was liberalized to allow workers to claim in advance of contributions: a step undertaken strictly as an emergency measure. The emergency, however, was not as short-lived as anticipated. Throughout the subsequent decade, discretionary benefit under various labels – 'uncovenanted', 'extended', 'transitional' –

allowed those who had no statutory right to state help to continue to claim it. Every year, fresh legislation defined new rights for specified periods, each concession being explained as a temporary measure necessitated by exceptional circumstances. As a result, previously agreed assumptions about who should 'count' as unemployed were drawn into question; the whole issue was thrown open to political debate.

Leaving the political parties aside, it is possible to distinguish four main groups in the early 1920s with strong opinions about how unemployment should be defined. At one extreme, the TUC argued that the government should be obliged to provide either work or full maintenance to all who needed it, and that the taxpayer be required to foot the bill. At the opposite extreme, the Treasury, the City of London and other financial interests saw unemployment as essentially a problem of wages. In modern parlance, workers were pricing themselves out of jobs; hence the export trades were failing and unemployment was rising. The solution was to be found in the restoration of the pound sterling as the world's main trading currency, a vital prerequisite to the revival of trade, which had been sadly disrupted by hyperinflation and political unrest in central Europe. This revaluation of the currency required strict controls on levels of public expenditure. If unemployment benefits were to be extended, therefore, industry must pay for the privilege.

Accordingly, industrial contributions to the unemployment insurance fund rose from 8d (*c.* 3p) to 1s 7d (*c.* 8p) between 1920 and 1922. Not surprisingly, this produced loud protests from the industrial employers. While the National Confederation of Employers' Organizations (NCEO) generally sympathized with the Treasury's line of argument, it did not accept the Treasury's solution. Just like the CBI in the mid-1980s, the NCEO claimed that national insurance contributions (NICs) raised industrial costs, making British exports uncompetitive and thus raising the incidence of unemployment. The real solution, the employers argued, lay in a return to the principles of 1911. Industry was willing to support those workers temporarily surplus to requirements, but had no automatic duty to support all the idle under all circumstances. The identity of the *bona fide* unemployed should be determined by the individual's contributory record. Those who failed to qualify for benefit should be referred to the poor law, whose administration should be removed from the hands of corrupt Labour guardians and returned to its original deterrent principles. This would restore work incentives and allow wages to fall in line with market values.

It should perhaps be noted that not all employers accepted this line. The Federation of British Industry (FBI), which was more representative of newer industries and the 'sheltered' (non-export) trades, sympathized with those members of the union movement who favoured 'insurance by industry', allowing each sector to develop its own benefit system in keeping with differing practices of labour management. This was because the national scheme forced the sheltered trades to subsidize the costs of unemployment in the export sector. When reducing or redefining their labour forces, new industries – in chemicals or food processing, for example – could afford to be reasonably generous. In the interwar years it was this sector which initiated redundancy or severance pay for workers cast adrift by the recession.

The notion that the poor law should pay for the problems of manufacturing industry, as advocated by the NCEO, was not popular at local level. No local politician was going to support a solution that promised to increase the already considerable burden imposed by the unemployed on the rates. Treatment under the poor law varied considerably from area to area, reflecting in part local tradition, in part electoral pressures and in part the degree of support for (and success of) the NUWM. The influence of the Labour Party at local level was reflected in the more generous levels of help given to the jobless, which contrasted with the prewar years. Local solutions, however, depended on the viability of local resources. Public works and decent relief had to be paid for out of the rates and with unemployment overwhelmingly concentrated in working-class districts, local initiatives of this type forced the poor to pay for the poorest. Further, high rates drove away potential industrial investment and thus made a bad position worse in the longer term. For this reason, the problems of the depressed areas proved incapable of local solution and local Labour parties came to support the line promoted by their Tory opponents, that unemployment should be considered a national charge. Indeed, the very experience of unemployment and its consequences in eroding the autonomy of local government did more than anything else to convert the Labour Party to the merits of national management and central control.

In the absence of any common agreement between these various political positions, policies shaping unemployment relief remained in a state of flux throughout the 1920s and well into the following decade. Periods of claim and rights of access were redefined at least once a year, sometimes twice. As a result, the identification of the unemployed no longer rested on the impersonal 'morality of mathematics', which had been the case under a purely contributory system. Instead, the issue was opened up to the vagaries of political compromise, at both local and national levels. Of course, the right to unemployment benefit did not itself determine who 'counted' as unemployed. Most poor law guardians insisted that unemployed claimants on relief continue to register at the exchanges. However, those losing any right to benefit or relief were less liable to see themselves as victims of recession and were therefore less likely to register at the exchanges. This 'discouraged worker syndrome' – to use its modern label – was most noticeable among non-heads of households who, by the end of the decade, were having the most difficulty in establishing any right to extended state support.

Within this broad framework, it is possible to discern how trends in policy changed in the interwar years in such a way as to alter public understanding about the scope and nature of unemployment, and the degree to which the unemployed should be held responsible for their own plight. In the early 1920s, as already indicated, unemployment policy tended to accommodate the demands of organized labour. Exchequer subsidies were available for the establishment of public works; benefit levels were raised, dependents' allowances introduced and periods of access extended – much to the fury of the NCEO. By the middle of the decade, however, the pendulum had begun to swing the other way. The Blanesburgh Committee, appointed in 1925 to review the situation, attempted to restore the insurance principle (although legislation implementing the report ultimately ducked the issue). The administration of discretionary regulations determining access to extended benefits was tightened. Even so, by the end of the 1920s, the problem of 'long term' unemployment – a concept unacknowledged before the First World War – had found its way into policy debates. The definition of unemployment was no longer founded upon the abstraction of actuarial calculation. This was to prove the lasting legacy of the interwar years.

By and large, the new definition of unemployment was fashioned to appease the political demands of the most powerful and vocal groups in the labour market. By contrast, unorganized and more marginal elements appear not to have benefited much from any extension in public largesse. Changes in official regulations encouraged the sharing of work. Those able to negotiate their working practices accordingly (either individually or collectively) could 'top up' earnings reduced by short-time or casual working with unemployment benefit. This could be seen on the docks, in some cotton mills, in textile engineering, hosiery, carpets, some areas of coalmining and a variety of other trades. In January 1927, two out of every three 'unemployed' cotton workers and one out of three 'unemployed' miners were actually working short-time. The same year, the secretary of the Dyers' Bleachers' and Finishers' Union boasted that, through the careful negotiation of working practices, they were 'carrying' a 60 per cent labour surplus in their trade.

Women workers, by contrast, became the chief target for official parsimony. Their claims were disqualified in large numbers; both their availability for work and their willingness to seek it were continuously drawn into question. Women were the chief target for the means test introduced in 1921, which disqualified claims to extended benefit from workers in households with someone in work. After 1922, when definitions of what constituted a 'suitable' job offer were revised, women claimants were offered domestic service jobs by the exchanges. This presented something of a Catch 22. If the offer was refused, the woman was disqualified because she had refused work. If it was accepted, she left the insurance scheme because domestic service was not an 'insured trade'. And, over and above this treatment, unknown numbers of women workers in intermittent employment with unco-operative employers failed to meet the requirements of the scheme's continuity rules and were disqualified from benefit.

Contrary to the assumptions of some economic historians, the incidence of irregular work did not disappear from Britain during the First World War. Although the history of unemployment in the interwar years is dominated by the structural problems of the export trades, there is every sign that work patterns commonly associated with the Edwardian era did not vanish, but survived in modified form, shored up by the judicious provision of public works. As the recession deepened in 1930, the Ministry of Labour *Gazette* found short-time working affecting up to 50 per cent of workers in wool textiles, carpets, boots and shoes, clothing, while only a few of these people were being returned as 'unemployed' at the exchanges. The use of short-time was geographically concentrated in the midlands, Lancashire and Yorkshire, where it was widespread in many industrial sectors. It was also common in south Wales, in both tinplate works and the mines. Even in the late 1930s, the Pilgrim Trust enquiry into the depressed areas found underemployment and casualism were still rife in centres like Liverpool, where they had always been common. As Beveridge pointed out to the Royal Commission on Unemployment Insurance in 1931, all the varieties of unemployment that investigators had revealed in Edwardian cities were still to be found during the Slump. The official statistics give a spurious impression. Unemployment was not a uniform experience and the numbers officially returned by the exchanges represented an arbitrary selection of those who lost work in the recession.

The advent of the Slump meant that, in the regions of industrial decline, intermittent employment became even more intermittent and in a growing proportion of cases was transformed into total redundancy. The Wall Street crash of 1929, the ensuing collapse of world trade and the financial crisis that hit the British government in 1931 all eventually led to unemployment policies far more in keeping with the NCEO's line of thought than those characterizing the previous decade. Insurance was returned to an actuarial basis and benefit levels were cut by 10 per cent. Those who had exhausted their right to benefit were to receive transitional payments, which was an Exchequer-funded form of relief administered through the local Public Assistance Committees (PACs), which had taken over from the Boards of Guardians in 1929. In 1934, the system was changed again and the administration of help to long-term claimants passed to the Unemployment Assistance Board (UAB). New regulations cut the right to benefit of married women and other non-household heads, a move affecting the status of young people. Although the new system was not as stringent as the NCEO would have liked, it did represent the final demise of the trade union demand for subsistence level benefits available as of right to all in search of work.

The hallmark of TUC policy in the 1930s was its lack of success. The industrial labour movement failed to break the hold of economic orthodoxy over the Labour government of 1929–31, failed to secure the introduction of retirement pensions or the raising of the school leaving age, failed to protect either benefit rates or access to them for the long-term unemployed, failed, indeed, to promote any union policies designed to alleviate unemployment or secure industrial recovery. The object of the struggles that had characterized the previous decade had been to secure state benefits for those out of work outside the context of the hated poor law. Under the reforms introduced in 1931 and 1934 long-term claimants were returned to less eligibility and the household means test. Although, as a sop to labour feeling, this group was still referred to as 'unemployed', for most the unemployment assistance official was indistinguishable from the poor law relieving officer in all but name.

When these changes were introduced, there was instant uproar. The Hunger Marches of 1932, 1934 and 1936 all bore eloquent testimony to the unjust and demeaning way in which the system operated. Respectable workers were suddenly subject to official interrogation and inspection like paupers. Through the process of surveillance and assessment, the unemployed were instructed, by reward and denial, on how to manage their affairs on a tightly limited budget. This methodology had been developed in an era which understood unemployment as a problem of individual morality. Surveillance of paupers had been considered an appropriate discipline for the casual 'residuum', the rough, spendthrift, drunken, dissolute, mendicant and lazy, whose habits had been frowned on by co-operative and chapel at least as much as by middle-class moralists. It was personally humiliating for skilled men to be associated with the dross of the labour market and their protest was as much about social injustice as it was about their newly reduced circumstances.

For reduced they most certainly were. In the previous decade, claiming benefit had been a matter of all or nothing. Benefit could be disallowed to those in breach of regulations – for refusing work or quitting voluntarily or whatever. It could not, however, be reduced; in this respect the system before 1931 had retained some of the characteristics of an insurance scheme, contributions being made to safeguard against a specific risk. Except in a handful of cases, there was no assessment of means involved. From 1931, this changed. The household resources of the long-term unemployed were taken into account in calculating the amount of relief allowed. Grown men became partially or fully dependent on the earnings of their children, even on the lodger's rent. In Walter Greenwood's *Love on the Dole* – written in the mid-1930s – we read of an unemployed coal-miner, his savings eroded by years of short-time working, together with his redundant son and his wife, all becoming dependent on the wages of his teenage daughter who worked short-time at the local mill. A man living with his parents in the Forest of Dean at this time recalled:

> Any family unlucky enough to have one of their number unemployed were forced to accept a lower standard of living because they had a passenger to carry. In our family I became the passenger. My benefit was immediately cut [by the means test] to 5/- [25p] a week. My father was paid on production at the coal face. When his earnings rose a little, the benefit was correspondingly reduced. The Means Test man went regularly to the office at the mine to find out how much my father was earning so these adjustments could be made.[1]

The new system was manifestly unfair. Apart from introducing positive disincentives to work hard, as illustrated above, it also operated in a very uneven manner. Local PACs kept to local precedent in assessing cases, which meant that disallowances varied wildly from one part of the country to another. An official survey in 1933 asked local authorities to assess ten 'specimen' cases. The results were predictably haphazard. At one extreme, total assistance in West Ham came to £12 11s 0d (£12.55) while at the other end of the scale, Blackpool offered only £3 12s 6d (£3.63), displaying the tight-fisted approach typical of the Lancashire poor law. While Rotherham offered the full rate of assistance in 98 per cent of cases, nearly 35 per cent of Birmingham's claimants were refused any help at all. In Cardiff alone, the assessment of identical cases could vary by over 100 per cent depending on which part of the city the claimant lived. The creation of the UAB in 1934, which took the long-term unemployed off the hands of the PACs, was supposed to iron out such irregularities. In the event, it did nothing of the sort. The introduction of national scales helped claimants in Lancashire and east Scotland, but it reduced relief rates elsewhere, notably in the north-east and south Wales. The resulting outcry shook the government into passing legislation that allowed the unemployed to claim either on UAB or PAC scales, whichever was the higher. Hence discrepancies remained.

The means test was not the only instrument used to cut costs; all regulations covering access were applied in a stricter fashion after 1931. Closer surveillance and interrogation were designed to discover the 'real' unemployed and to detect the fraudulent. Max Cohen recalled his appearance before the Court of Referees, referred as being in breach of the regulation requiring the applicant to be capable of obtaining his livelihood through insurable employment (a requirement, one might be forgiven for thinking, that said more about the availability of jobs than it did about the claimant's working capacities).

> What matters to them (the Court) was the impression they received of you. If they thought you were a 'decent chap' this would weigh with them in any doubtful case as much as any more technical aspect. . . . For really, boiling it all down, you were completely at their mercy.[2]

The new system was particularly hard on female claimants. Under the 1931 Anomalies Act, a married woman was disqualified from *all* benefit unless she could show a 'reasonable expectation' of obtaining insurable employment, and that her chances were not affected by the fact of her marriage. In cotton textiles, pottery work, hosiery, boots and shoes, women still continued work after marriage. Women provided the bulk of the workforce in food-processing, tobacco trades, retail, catering and the chemical industry, and some of these were married. Under the new regulations, the closure of the local mill disqualified all married female textile workers from benefit. The miner whose pit had closed ten years before would still be accepted as 'unemployed' while the newly redundant pottery or textile worker would not, by virtue of her sex and marital status. The consequence was poverty in areas of Lancashire where wages were low because the traditional household economy of the unskilled depended on two wage packets, not one. Between 1931 and 1933 nearly a quarter of a million claims were disallowed under this regulation alone; this figure does not include numbers disqualified for not being 'available for work' because they were tied down by domestic commitments.[3]

Stricter administration had its own rationale. Much as in the 1970s and 1980s, officials claimed that the unemployed were making insufficient effort to find work. The provision of benefits was keeping wages artificially high and allowing the idle to malinger at the country's expense. Disallowing benefit would solve the problem by forcing the 'voluntary' unemployed back into the labour market, making them accept less attractive jobs at lower wages. In the 1930s, Whitehall became obsessed with the problem of 'wage overlap'. Unemployed men with large families, it was claimed, were able to get more money by remaining on state benefit than they could earn from a job in their previous trade. A crude form of 'wage stop' was introduced to prevent this. Although the problem applied only to a tiny minority, assumptions about scrounging and fears that the unemployed would 'settle' on the dole continued to plague official circles. In the spring of 1931, the Ministry of Labour investigated the circumstances of a sample of 2,354 disallowed claimants from eight different industrial areas. Far from discovering habitual malingering, the enquiry revealed widespread confusion over the maze of rules governing rights of access and bitterness in the minds of many at the apparent injustice of their treatment. Disallowance did not force a return to work, but marked another step on the road to abject poverty and despair. The Ministry reported:

> The picture is not, in the main, a cheerful one. There is ample evidence of suffering, some of it bound up with a pre-existing state of poverty; some of it directly due to disallowance. Half the married men in the sample fell into destitution and, generally, the other half only subsisted under grave economic

difficulties. Relations and friends were a standby for all classes in the sample, but in that case the trouble was not banished; it was only spread. Others than the disallowed persons had to make sacrifices and many were encumbered with arrears of rent and debts. In spite of efforts, regular employment, either in industry or on relief works, was usually unobtainable. At this dark side of the picture no one need be surprised.[4]

Stricter surveillance did not reveal a mass of fraudulent claims. Neither official nor unofficial surveys discovered claimants who managed to play the system to their advantage. What they did discover was poverty, among employed and unemployed alike. In the 1930s, the unemployed in general, especially the long-term cases, were particularly vulnerable. Estimates of the proportion of unemployed families in poverty varied from 41 per cent (the Pilgrim Trust) to four out of every five claimants on the UAB. For long-term cases, the incidence was very severe. In February 1936, in the course of his research for *The Road to Wigan Pier*, George Orwell met 'Paddy Grady, an unemployed miner. A tall lean man about 35, intelligent and well informed . . . He is a single man getting 17/- [*c.* 83p] a week and is in a dreadful state physically from years of underfeeding and idleness. His front teeth are almost entirely rotted away.'[5]

Poverty was widespread among large families. The threat of wage overlap was real for some in this group, especially chronic casuals, and this reflected the degree of poverty among those ostensibly in work (but probably on short-time) as well. The situation led some nutrition experts – with support from the British Medical Association – to argue that it was not possible to raise healthy children on the scales of assistance given by the government. This provoked controversy. Higher PAC and UAB rates threatened to exacerbate the problem of wage overlap as well as increasing levels of public expenditure, which the Conservative administration of the mid-1930s was so eager to contain. Hence the Ministry of Health tended to ignore evidence of malnutrition and ill-health. Surveys of the unemployed in Europe and the United States exposed the high incidence of psychological depression and illness among the unemployed; in Britain, around one-third of the rising numbers of claimants for sickness benefit were probably struck down by 'nervous' disorders. Routine medical inspection identified 21 per cent of children in Pontypridd as malnourished: unemployment in the town stood at 58 per cent. Compared with the Continent, the British unemployed and their families escaped relatively lightly. Surveys in Poland showed that half of all miners' and a third of all weavers' children could not attend school for lack of clothes. In Austria, 57 per cent of the children of the Viennese unemployed were underweight for their age.

The political legacy of the 1930s – the 'devil's decade' according to Claude Cockburn – became fully apparent during the Second World War. The advent of war once again transformed labour surplus into chronic labour shortage; the long-term unemployed from the coal-mines and shipyards found their services again in demand. Men very recently deemed 'unemployable' were reintegrated into the labour force, along with others who had previously been categorized as sick, disabled and vagrant (and therefore unfit for work). Mass evacuation of children from the inner cities to the relatively prosperous country towns brought home the consequences of the Slump in a way that all the surveys and reports on the depressed areas had never been able to do. In this way, the hated 'means test man' entered the nation's demonology. The groundswell of popular support which greeted the publication of the Beveridge Report on social insurance and allied services in 1942 illustrates this point. The chief merit in Beveridge's proposals for many people lay in his promise to give benefit 'as of right' for all interruptions in earnings 'from the cradle to the grave'. Means testing was to be no more. With hindsight we can see that this prediction was wildly optimistic. The return of mass unemployment in the 1970s and 1980s saw the assessment of means re-established as the mainstay of state help for the unemployed.

Conclusions: redefining unemployment in the 1980s

When we step back from the administrative minutiae governing rights to state unemployment benefits, we can see how the concept of unemployment changed in response to the prevailing political climate. In the 1920s, when access to reasonably generous levels of benefit could be regarded as a privilege, those thrown out of work by the recession fought to be included in this category, with varying degrees of success. In general, unorganized or marginal workers, women and those in less than perfect health did not do so well as unionized trades where working agreements could be negotiated to allow maximum numbers to stay 'in benefit'. In the 1930s, the picture changed. Some short-time and casual workers managed to conform to contributory regulations and retained access to benefit 'as of right'. Indeed, in contrast to the requirements of the 1911 scheme, the contributory regulations were much relaxed.[6] For long-term claimants, however, the whole notion of insurance became irrelevant and, with this, the advantages of being labelled 'unemployed' disappeared. Labour market rejects tended to transfer to other categories of social dependency. By the early 1930s, administration had reverted to earlier principles of deterrence in order to weed out elements unlikely ever to work again in an insured trade, who were thereby reclassified as disabled, ill or 'retired' from waged employment. While such reshuffling might appear to be a realistic response to severe recession, we have to question whether those officially classified as 'unemployed' represent the total numbers of those who lost work in the interwar period.

What the state was doing throughout this period was using the right to benefit as the means to restructure the labour market in accordance with social norms and the changing nature of labour demand. However, politicians and public officials continued to understand unemployment as a uniform experience, and to design state schemes accordingly. This was explained in terms of equality of treatment and natural justice. However, the imposition of a single set of regulations on diverse working practices did not – could not – have this effect. Looking behind the official statistics, we find some casuals and short-time workers, albeit a minority, accepted as 'unemployed', while many more were not. Underemployment remained very widespread; loss of work was just as 'real' for the coal-miner working three days out of six as it was for his colleague who was on unemployment benefit for two weeks in every four. The difference was that the latter could claim state benefits while the former, in all probability, could not. When viewed from this perspective, we can see how uniform regulations operated in an arbitrary and unfair fashion – while giving us a distorted and partial picture of the extent of job loss during the recession.

Thanks to the changing political climate, and the varying ways in which the partially employed were taken into account, it becomes difficult to know whether the official unemployment figures tell us very much about the impact of the depression on job loss at all. Both the industrial and political constructions of unemployment varied from place to place and over time. If the recession of 1921–2 had occurred fifteen years later, for example, it would have had far less impact in terms of numbers 'unemployed' and numbers assisted. Access to state help was far tighter. The process of categorization is not as self-evident as is frequently assumed; unemployment was then, as now, politically defined.

A similar process of readjustment has taken place in recent years. Again, tighter administration and lower insurance benefits aim to push the unemployed back on to the labour market, thereby driving down wages. In 1982–3, the value of unemployment insurance benefit was cut when the earnings related elements were removed and the whole became liable to tax. Although rates of benefit are linked by law to the cost of living, from 1986 uprating for the unemployed has operated at the discretion of the Secretary of State. Overall, the real value of unemployment benefits fell by an estimated 20 per cent between 1979 and 1987. Unlike the interwar years, which witnessed a relaxation in contributory regulations, legislation passed in 1988 has raised the contributory requirement for claimants from one tax year to two. In the interwar years, 'voluntary quits' were punished by a six-week disqualification from benefit. In 1986 and 1988, this was extended twice; now, such cases cannot claim benefit for six months and are allowed only 40 per cent of the full rate of means tested relief (now called income support). If the rules governing insurance benefit operating in 1978–9 had been extant in 1988, the Exchequer would have paid £500 million more to the unemployed.

At the same time, large numbers have been excluded from benefit through the extension of part-time work. Although a thirty-five-hour week is considered normal, anyone working up to twenty-seven hours is officially a part-timer and, as such, is not covered by national insurance and so cannot claim benefit 'as of right' when initially unemployed. And the 'availability for work' clause – then as now the catch-all for disqualifying female claimants – has recently been made more stringent. From 1987, to be accepted as 'available for work', a mother must show that she can get full-time child care for a pre-school child (part-time for the over fives) within twenty-four hours and the child-minder must not be a relative (on the grounds that such a person might collude in a false claim). In 1987, 107,000 disallowances resulted from this regulation alone. In 1988–9, more attention is being given to the criteria governing offers of 'suitable' work, with a view to stricter surveillance. As in the interwar years, claimants must demonstrate that they have been actively seeking work, even when they know that none is available. It is hardly any wonder that the Thatcher government declared its total opposition to the Social Charter, sponsored by the EEC in 1989, with its emphasis on equal treatment for the sexes and the provision of earnings-related systems of social support. If forced to conform to international standards, the government's position on unemployment benefits would have to be completely revised, at considerable cost and with the likely consequence of the official figures, carefully massaged into respectability in the late 1980s, rising to their earlier levels.

These changes have forced the unemployed and their families back on to means-tested benefits, to top up – or substitute for – adequate national insurance. Levels of benefit available 'as of right' are the lowest in Europe and access to them is more difficult now than ever before. If Beveridge could witness the fate of the insurance scheme he helped found in the 1940s, he would not recognize it as his own. Far from leading the world with its schemes of social insurance, Britain now boasts one of the harshest and most stigmatizing systems of social security in the western industrial economies.

The rhetoric surrounding these changes has a familiar ring. Now (as then) we are informed that, given the chance, the unemployed will malinger indefinitely at public expense. For economic recovery to work, industry must become more competitive. Costs – labour costs – must be reduced and high levels of benefit will only encourage workers to price themselves out of jobs. If life on the dole

is made uncomfortable enough, the unemployed will start competing actively in the job market and wages will be encouraged to fall.
Folk memory is short. The 1930s demonstrated that disallowances
and means testing do not drive workers into jobs but drive their
families into destitution. Once again, the poverty debates are being
revived, and once again Whitehall is sceptical about the existence of
a problem while independent investigators reach very different
conclusions. It would be foolhardy to say that history repeats itself.
Even so, the claim that things are quite different (implying better)
now than they were then is too frequently made by those who have
little idea what they are talking about to be completely credible.

V

State Training and Employment Policies

Introduction

Both in the past and in the present, the extent of unemployment has been magnified either because those looking for workers and those seeking jobs have remained in ignorance of each other's existence, or because employers require skills and experience that the unemployed do not possess. Hence public policy, at both local and national level, has been concerned to improve the quality of labour available and to promote its mobility between different sectors. These activities can be justified in a number of ways. Most obviously, a positive policy can raise levels of economic performance and help restructure the economy by encouraging the effective deployment of manpower and raising the levels of skill and adaptability among job-seekers. This strategy would require a total manpower policy to be successful, not simply programmes for the unemployed alone. In the second place, training the unemployed allows those surplus to current requirements in one sector to regain their independence by becoming skilled in another. Training therefore prevents the 'deterioration' of the unemployed as well as promoting investment in human capital for future economic needs.

Finally, and closely allied to this, training need not involve the acquisition of skills at all. 'Training' is a term quite commonly used to refer to the imposition of work discipline on the idle. In other words, government training schemes serve to allay the irritation commonly provoked by the thought that some people are able to live at the public's expense without having to stir a finger to earn their keep. Such sentiments, illustrated in the following quotation from *The Times* date from the interwar period, but could easily have been published in recent years:

> There are hundreds and thousands of young men who do not show any disposition to bestir themselves to get out of unemployment into employment . . . there is a slackness of moral fibre and of will as of muscle . . . salutary action is beyond dispute. The breakdown of morale can only be made good by applying compulsion.[1]

In this instance the paper was advocating that the UAB stop unemployment assistance to all who refused a place on a government training programme. The idea that the long-term unemployed be required to accept a place on a training scheme as a condition of benefit has been revived in the late 1980s. 'Workfare' has been depicted as a new idea whose origins are to be found in the United States. This is far from being the case. The notion that the unemployed should work for their keep has received attention off and on for a very long time. The principle was embodied in the old poor law of Elizabeth I; twentieth-century advocates of such schemes have included politicians as far apart as Sir Alfred Mond (in 1927) and Francis Pym, senior cabinet minister in the first two Thatcher administrations.

Training policies for the unemployed have had to serve a variety of ends. In attempting to do this, there has been a tendency for official programmes to fall between two stools. If they promote 'real' training in marketable skills they are criticized for trying to make a silk purse out of a sow's ear. The unemployed are the rejects of the labour market and thus the element least likely to give the nation a good return on its investment in human capital. Further, government trainees will compete for jobs with those trained by the private sector – and may well be regarded as second rate by comparison. For there is the more general argument, adopted by those who believe in the virtues of the free market, that government should not involve itself in this area anyway. Industry knows the skills it requires and industry will train accordingly. This attitude is not only found on the management side. Trade unions also have long looked askance at state training programmes, seeing them as the means by which capitalism undermines wage rates and bargaining power by flooding the market with cheap labour.

If, on the other hand, government training is used as a polite euphemism for what was once called 'setting the able-bodied poor to work', then a different but related set of contradictions emerge. If 'workfare' is to be implemented, we have to decide what work the unemployed should do and what wages, if any, they should be paid for doing it. In both cases, there is a strong risk that extensive state activity will end up exacerbating the unemployment problem, not solving it. If the state sponsors jobs in areas where commercial interests are already active, it is likely that the agency operating with a public subsidy will offer a cheaper service than its commercial counterpart, and may drive the latter out of business. If firms and employers are paid to take on government 'trainees', then they may see this labour as a cheap alternative to taking on their own trainees and will cut their recruitment programme accordingly. If, on the other hand, the state funds public works, or projects under the Community Programme as this activity was called in the early 1980s, there is the objection that this does not prepare the unemployed for 'real' jobs in the 'real' market economy. They are only trained for work that no commercial undertaking would touch because it is inherently unprofitable. Such initiatives cannot realistically be characterized as 'training' at all; they are really short-term job creation programmes. And in both cases, if what the critics claim is true, state policy is failing in one of its primary aims: to alleviate the problem by restoring the unemployed to financial independence.

These arguments became fairly common in the discussions surrounding government training programmes in the 1970s and 1980s. A bewildering array of initiatives developed at this time, identified by strings of initials incomprehensible to all but those familiar with Manpower Services Commission (MSC) and all its works. Social investigation proliferated into the degree of job substitution, the rate of drop-out, the subsequent fate of trainees and so on. In the eyes of many, this was considered a new development, the first incursion by a British government into the field of manpower policy. In fact, as with state support for the unemployed, this is a time-honoured area of official intervention. Medieval guilds, with the backing of the law, laid down the training required of those who claimed mastership of a specific trade. They licensed practitioners and punished those who ignored their regulations. The corrosion of legal controls surrounding indentures, which had stipulated the duties of both master and apprentice, and the abolition of pauper apprentices in the early nineteenth century, both signified the passing of an old order, leaving the field open to commercial enterprise. State activity in training for work by the mid-nineteenth century was confined to the education of the young in the values of sobriety, thrift and industry. Subsequent attempts to extend the role of government into areas of 'real' training have met with much resistance. With the slow but persistent decline in Britain's industrial performance, we have become aware that British manpower policies are the most underdeveloped in Europe – and this is often used to explain underlying economic problems.

Training for work: an analysis of failure?

Lack of policy in this area, historically speaking, cannot be attributed to any absence of initiative. From the late nineteenth century, numerous public enquiries and reports bewailed the poor quality of a state education system which gave little emphasis to the applied sciences or to the development of those technical skills vital to the promotion of new production methods and thus to industrial prosperity. Many, casting their eyes overseas, stressed the inferiority of British education when contrasted to other countries in Europe, particularly Germany. There, technical schools and colleges sent a never-ending stream of well-trained and competent engineers and technicians to the aid of German industry well in excess of anything the antiquated British apprenticeship system could produce. In the late nineteenth century, steps were taken to remedy the situation. As industrial rivalry between the two countries intensified, British reformers took a growing interest in German training and industrial methods with the view to beating the rival at his own game.

Certainly, the last quarter of the nineteenth century witnessed a burst of activity to remedy the situation. In 1878, five major City of

London Livery companies created the City and Guilds of London Institute for the Advancement of Technical Education, which initiated its own examinations in technical subjects. The following decade saw the creation of new red-brick universities and the first polytechnics: the British attempt to reproduce their own version of the large technological universities founded in France and Germany earlier in the century. In 1890, excise duty on alcohol was earmarked – a rather bizarre development – for the promotion of vocational education. Local authorities received central subsidies to further the establishment of colleges of further education, in co-operation with local employers. These provided block release and sandwich courses relevant to the local economy. 'Whisky money' supplemented other grant moneys available from the Science and Art Department of the Privy Council, which had been sponsoring courses in technology and design since the 1830s. And there are signs that local initiatives of this nature served employers well, allowing them a prominent role in determining the nature of training and access to courses. Although this meant that local provision was only as innovatory as local industry allowed it to be, it does imply that we should not take the complaints of would-be reformers too much at face value.

Even so, the greater part of public investment in education at the turn of the century was concerned with the promotion of docility and obedience, not technological competence. Before 1870, a network of voluntary and charitable schools had been almost the sole resource from which working-class children could acquire basic literary and numerical skills. The churches formed the backbone of this voluntary movement and the association between religious foundation and elementary education remained strong. Knowledge of scripture and catechism, with their emphasis on teaching the child his place in the natural order, took precedence over the development of practical abilities. The state-run elementary schools introduced in 1870 aimed to extend, not replace, the existing system. It was not until after the turn of the century that local authorities were legally permitted to fund schools providing anything more than very basic elementary education, and even then the provision of secondary places was very sparse and patchy.

Dissatisfaction with this state of affairs was widespread. Improved industrial training was considered central to the promotion of national efficiency, which was being widely advocated at this time. Support for the establishment of more sophisticated forms of state education came from political parties of all complexions. Education and training formed part of the main discussions on labour market reform: as vital to the elimination of casualism as the modernization of production techniques and the protection of Britain's imperial interests. Beveridge saw retraining as an essential step in the reintegration of those workers jettisoned by decasualization. As such, it formed a central component in the 'scientific' rationalization of the labour market and the promotion of social reform. Particularly prominent in the area were Robert Morant, Permanent Secretary at the Board of Education and Sydney Webb, leader of the influential Fabians. Morant and Webb between them secured the passage of the 1902 Education Act, which tidied up the administration of state education and allowed (but did not require) the newly created local education authorities (LEAs) to raise rates for the provision of secondary schools, including technical schools and colleges. Webb had long been interested in the potential of state education as a ladder of social mobility, which would allow the gifted working-class child to develop his full potential, including access to university education if need be. The creation of a meritocracy necessitated an education system that recognized a wider range of talents than those intellectual qualities traditionally recognized by the establishment. Technical ability merited equal recognition with more academic skills.

The view that the state should promote more technical and scientific education among schoolchildren has been reiterated with monotonous regularity throughout the twentieth century. The 1918 Education Act advocated the establishment of technical schools and, until the requirement was abandoned in the early 1920s, insisted on the provision of day release or continuation classes for the fourteen- to sixteen-year-olds who were already in work. The provision of technical schools at post-elementary level was again recommended by both the Spens and Hadow reports (in 1926 and 1936 respectively) in the interwar years. They also found their way into Butler's 1944 Education Act, but never actually appeared in the flesh, so to speak. In the mid-1980s, the same ideas were taken off the shelf, dusted down and presented (as 'new' initiatives, naturally) to the public in the shape of the Technical and Vocational Training Initiative (TVEI) (a training programme to be run within existing secondary schools) and the introduction of twenty City Technical Colleges. These colleges, aimed at the eleven–eighteen-year-olds with a bent for science and techology, are the 1980s equivalent of the type of school Webb and Butler were advocating generations ago. The difference is that these are to be sponsored by industry, not the LEAs. Whether or not this will bring them the success that evaded their forebears remains a matter for conjecture. The precedents, however, are not encouraging.

Early twentieth-century reformers were not only interested in the promotion of universal secondary education and the provision of a technical component in the school curriculum. They were as concerned with the problem of the young worker as any of their counterparts in recent years. The problem then was, however, slightly different. It was not so much that school leavers were prone to unemployment; rather, they tended to go straight into 'dead-end' or 'blind alley' jobs as boy labour which they lost as soon as they reached adulthood. Errand boys, office boys, messengers and page boys all typified the type of work involved. These were supplemented by spurious 'apprentices', who were widely used by unscrupulous employers as cheap labour while they were young enough, being discarded once they reached an age when they could command an adult rate. The problem was essentially male; girls were still largely sent into domestic service before marriage. These boys, however, formed the pool from which Beveridge and others considered the future casual 'residuum' would be recruited. According to the Minority Report of the Royal Commission on the Poor Laws: 'thousands of boys, from the lack of any sort of training for industrial occupations, grow up, almost inevitably, so as to become chronically unemployed or underemployed and presently to recruit the ranks of the unemployable. In Glasgow recently nearly 20 per cent of the labourers in distress are under the age of 25'.[2]

Similar condemnations can be found in the writings of Beveridge, Rowntree, the Webbs and in the speeches of Winston Churchill. All of them agreed that such exploitation represented a waste of manpower resources, perpetuated the oversupply of unskilled casual labourers and should be stopped. The answer was to be found in the provision of a careers advisory service to place young lads in proper training for skilled work. The Juvenile (Choice of Employment) Act was passed by Parliament in 1911; this established advisory services for young people in labour exchanges all round the country. Even so, observers in the 1930s found that little had changed. Industrialists in mining, metals and engineering were still operating a 'relay' system, replacing eighteen-year-olds with fourteen-year-old school leavers, while in distribution, transport and communication the use of messenger, delivery and van boys was still common. Such practices still prompted the condemnation of the authorities in terms identical to those used twenty years earlier. It was, however, only in the aftermath of the Second World War, when juvenile wage rates were raised and labour shortages were chronic, that such practices disappeared.

The history of official efforts to secure the improvement of technical training among the young has a highly repetitive tone. Like the labour exchanges' efforts to secure the more efficient distribution of work, state policy to further training and structure careers secured only marginal change. Reform seems to have been singularly ineffective and it is as well that we understand why. The government was not trying to tackle labour market problems in a manner radically different from methods used in other countries. As already noted, German technical training, run by the state, was the envy of the world. And all over the Continent, especially in major cities in Belgium, Germany and France, labour registries and bureaux were far more effective in securing the co-ordination of labour supply and demand than the British exchanges ever were. Throughout the twentieth century, Britain's manpower policies have lagged well behind those of its European rivals. The reasons for this lie in the structure of British industry and in the controls imposed on the market by systems of collective bargaining which had established themselves in the course of the nineteenth century, and which were particularly well developed in skilled sectors. National schemes to rationalize employment and raise skill levels signified a move by the government into territory already colonized, at least in part, by both sides of industry. This area has been one of dispute ever since and this has remained one of the chief reasons for the 'backward' nature of British manpower policies.

Industrialization in Britain was a singularly slow process, spread out over more than a century; *laisser faire* economic orthodoxy meant little control had been exercised by the state over the direction or pace of change. By contrast, industrialization in Germany had been concentrated into a much shorter space of time and had taken place with the direct encouragement of the German government. Thanks to this prolonged gestation, nineteenth-century British industry tended to be small in scale and technologically diffuse in nature. By the end of the nineteenth century, British engineering firms were much smaller on average than their German counterparts. Some had adapted the latest production techniques, others had not, preferring to rely on the skills of their workforce in the manufacture of a wide range of products which were made to order, not for stock. Even after the First World War, British firms showed little inclination to adopt the mass production techniques widely used in the United States. As late as the 1930s, the growth of the car industry reflected traditional structures; the production of most components was subcontracted to a mass of small firms and were subsequently assembled by workers at Cowley or Longbridge. Such firms operated on limited budgets. As labour was plentiful, and cheap compared to the United States, there was little incentive to invest in the latest technology.

Mass production only really took off in Britain after the Second World War. As a result, the structure of British industry remained technologically diffuse and its management generally unprofessional. In short, management remained dubious about the advantages the provision of state training might bring and greeted proposals in this area with a mixture of opinions ranging from the indifferent to the hostile. As production processes, and therefore the required standards of skill, were so varied and heterogeneous, it made much more sense to train workers 'on the job': a traditional system which offered the added advantage of cheap labour in the shape of apprentices and trainees. Hence part of the problem stemmed from the disinclination of employers to take on state-trained products, which encouraged new recruits to enter industry by traditional means.

Employer indifference only makes up half the picture. State intervention in questions of employment and training was also resented by contemporary trade unions. Late nineteenth-century union organization was predominantly of skilled men; these had long sought to control recruitment to their trades as well as to determine working conditions within them. National unions in construction, shipbuilding, metal-working and engineering insisted that their members work only in 'legal' shops at 'legal' rates of pay, and this 'legality' depended, in some trades, on the employer's willingness to observe union stipulations concerning the ratio of apprentices to journeymen. The branch secretary acted virtually as a labour exchange, referring suitable members 'on the books' (out of work and claiming benefits) to employers in need of labour. The system worked generally to mutual advantage. Employers found it useful because union men knew their trade and the branch secretary understood the requirements needed for a job and the experience of his members in a way no labour exchange official could ever manage to do. In return for unemployment benefits, some unions, notably in the construction industries, required their members to 'tramp' from town to town in search of work, contacting the local branch to identify vacancies. Union journals carried reports about the state of trade all round the country. In this manner, some major unions, such as the Boilermakers on Clydeside in the early twentieth century, managed to control training in their section of the labour market and thus regulated access to jobs. A wide range of industrial agreements and trade practices, covering everything from manning levels to job demarcation, were designed to protect jobs. State-sponsored training therefore tended to be regarded with no little hostility as an attempt by government to undermine union organization by flooding the market with an inferior type of skilled workman.

Labour mistrust of state employment services was transformed into open hostility during the First World War. State-run labour exchanges were used to send women and juvenile 'dilutees' into engineering and munition works, to release fit skilled men for the dubious honour of serving in the trenches. Wartime restructuring undermined old systems of apprenticeship and reduced the status of the man who had served his time. Although David Lloyd George had committed himself to the restoration of prewar practices under the government's Treasury Agreement with the unions in 1915, escalating technological change rendered old controls largely redundant by the time of the Armistice. The circumstances of the war had given those who believed in state manpower policies as the means to raise industrial efficiency the chance to prove their case. The experiment was a failure. Government direction, far from providing solutions to industrial problems, tended to make matters worse. By the end of the war, labour, employers and even civil servants in Whitehall all agreed on a policy of restoring 'home rule for industry'. Industrial interests were best served by keeping state intervention to a minimum. The Barnes Committee's enquiries into employment exchanges after the Armistice exposed Beveridge's failure to appreciate the complexities of industrial structures and work specialization in his advocacy of rationalization. The exchanges were shunned by both sides of industry as placement agencies because they were insufficiently sensitive to industry's requirements.

In the aftermath of the war, government did sponsor an extensive Interrupted Apprenticeship Scheme for the returning soldiers. However, more extensive training initiatives foundered on the twin rocks of Treasury parsimony and industrial opposition. The centralized state-run system of technical instruction developed in Germany still excited admiration, but proved incapable of being transplanted on to British soil. Government training programmes for the unemployed remained very meagre. In the 1920s, those that existed concentrated their attention on the young in the depressed areas, with a view to transferring them to more prosperous parts of the country. By 1929, eleven government centres were handling about 3,500 trainees a year on courses in skilled metalwork, furnishing trades, gas and electrical engineering. The only major interwar injection of public funds into 'real' training developed in the late 1930s, when Government Training Centres (GTCs) were expanded to promote skills vital to the rearmament programme. Other efforts to train the unemployed concentrated on the type of 'training' that had been sponsored by the poor law: designed less to impart actual skills than to maintain morale, reinforce work discipline and prevent degeneration. Schemes were set up which involved the co-operation of the voluntary sector as well as the local authorities. Then as now, the main target group were young workers who might otherwise degenerate into long-term dependency on the social security system.

The interwar equivalent of the Youth Opportunities Programme (YOP) and the Youth Training Scheme (YTS) were the Juvenile Unemployment Centres (JUCs), which changed their name to Juvenile Instruction Centres (JICs) in 1930. Commonly referred to as 'dole schools' in the 1920s, the JUCs proved generally unpopular. Provision was patchy and attendance sporadic; only about a quarter of juvenile unemployed attended them at all and they did little more than provide physical exercise for the boys and domestic science classes for girls. After 1930, greater emphasis was placed on restoring employability and maintaining morale. Attendance became a compulsory condition for the receipt of state benefit and, after school leavers were incorporated into the unemployment insurance scheme (1934), attendance went up. In 1935, 188 JICs provided 191,000 places. This represented something of a peak and in the context of the lower incidence of juvenile unemployment in the interwar years bears comparison with recent attendance on YTS, which is also compulsory for the young unemployed. There, however, comparisons end: the JICs did not attempt to provide work experience but gave instruction in rudimentary skills. Both schemes, however, were more concerned to keep the young unemployed off the streets and out of trouble than to enhance the life chances of the recession's victims.

In similar vein, Transfer Instruction Centres (TICs) were established in 1928 to act as 'reconditioning' centres for those long-term unemployed who were, in the local exchange's opinion, making insufficient effort to find work. These were, essentially, labour camps to which men from the depressed areas were sent for a twelve-week stint of forestry work to 'tone them up' for transference or further training. As Margaret Bondfield (Minister of Labour) put it in February 1930, in a memorandum to the Cabinet:

There are a number of young men in the distressed areas who are very unlikely to obtain work either locally or elsewhere without some course of reconditioning, but who refuse to avail themselves of the offer of training . . . I think the stage has been reached in the process of 'draining the waterlogged areas' where such men should have their benefit disallowed if they refuse without good reason to take a course of instruction if offered to them.

In this case, disqualification only affected 1,800 claimants and was stopped after nine months. Even so, support for compulsion remained strong among local exchange officials; men continued to attend Instruction Centres (as TICs were renamed in the early 1930s) under the impression that their 'availability for work' would be questioned and their benefit disallowed if they refused. Nor was there any question that this 'training' provided marketable skills. As a paper prepared for the UAB in 1935 noted:

> The Instruction Centre is not, strictly speaking, a training centre at all. It is designed to tone-up the 'trainees' physical and moral condition and to teach or revive in him habits of punctuality and decency and a reasonable standard of discipline and to prove to him by experience that to leave home is not a disaster of the first magnitude.[3]

Or, as the UAB itself put it, more succinctly, 'The able-bodied poor are set to work, though in more recent years this phrase has been replaced by the euphemism of training.'[4]

Around 120,000 men passed through the ICs in the decade 1928–38, 7,000 more than attended the vocational GTCs. Of these, 25 per cent were dismissed or failed to complete the course and a further 60 per cent finished the course unplaced. The men slept in dormitories, herded together with no privacy. The work was hard and monotonous, the food in the camps highly unpalatable. The whole initiative was very unpopular among the unemployed themselves, who earned no allowance but whose families' unemployment assistance was docked five shillings (25p) while they were away, ostensibly to pay for their keep.

The notion of getting round the unemployment problem by transferring the young and mobile away from declining areas, especially the coalfields, had been a mainstay of public policy since the late 1920s, when the government had introduced advice, help and removal grants for young people willing to move south in search of work. Grants were made available by the Ministry of

Labour for training girls as domestic servants, to make good the servant shortage among middle-class households. In this area at least, official training schemes met with opposition from women's organizations, and from the girls themselves, some of whom were disinclined to accept their fate as a live-in skivvy. By the 1930s, poor health and low aptitude among the young who still remained in the depressed areas was reducing the efficacy of transference. Hence the efforts to force the issue by compulsory means for marginal cases. By the mid-1930s, economic growth in the midlands and south-east helped harden official attitudes towards those who insisted on remaining unemployed and at home. On the eve of the Second World War, there was renewed talk of compulsion but hostilities broke out before any initiative could be implemented.

In general, these schemes were not a roaring success. During the Slump, the demand for labour was hardly buoyant even in the midlands and south-east. People in Oxford and Bristol, for example, understandably resented the increased competition for jobs due to the influx of 'foreigners' from south Wales. Further, as state help concentrated on the young and mobile, those capable of being transferred out of depressed areas had a tendency to transfer themselves back again when a job fell through, or when homesickness and loneliness became too much to bear. Finally, we should recall that government was reinforcing an established migratory drift towards the south. Possibly a proportion of state-sponsored migrants found work. Many more did not and some extended their personal search so far that they took to the road permanently. The numbers of vagrants and tramps increased dramatically during the 1930s, for much the same reasons that they have done in the 1980s. As George Orwell demonstrated in *Down and out in Paris and London* (1933), a number of these were casualties of a job market that had no further need of their services. A policy designed to restore employability and promote mobility did nothing to expand the overall number of jobs on offer. At best, it could only promote the chances of one jobseeker at the expense of the rest.

The outbreak of war produced the familiar recriminations about the surfeit of unskilled workers on the labour market, the lack of engineers and technicians qualified to make, repair or operate the advanced machinery needed for the war, the poor educational standards common among British workers, which rendered them incapable of reading an instruction manual, assessing a technical drawing or understanding a spreadsheet. Once again, the promotion of technical education and the creation of the postwar Youth Employment Service were considered sufficient to remedy such defects. And once again, industry's preference for established recruitment and training procedures when wartime controls were removed rendered the new state initiatives marginal and ineffective. In the course of the 1950s, it became clear that Britain's manpower policies lagged far behind those found in Sweden, France and Germany.

By the 1960s, the question of skill shortages in key areas of future growth – and chronic underinvestment and overmanning in declining industries – appeared to threaten the country's economic future. This formed the context within which the Labour Party, under the leadership of Harold Wilson, revived ideas about a new compact between state and industry, including the area of industrial training, as part of a drive to prepare Britain for the 'white hot heat of the technological revolution'. In the event, this failed to produce more than a pale pink glow. It was not possible for a Labour administration to alienate the union movement by reducing the sphere of free collective bargaining which was so jealously guarded. The Industrial Training Board (ITBs), which were designed to let particular industries shape their own training schemes under state sponsorship, failed to win much support. By the mid-1980s, all but seven were scrapped. In 1973, the Conservative administration under Edward Heath decided to promote its own initiative, to succeed where Labour had failed, and introduced a new agency to promote and co-ordinate a more positive national manpower policy.

Thus was the Manpower Services Commission (MSC) born. Its brief was simple: to revamp government placement agencies and training schemes and to promote redeployment from declining to expanding sectors of the economy. In its early years, it appeared to revolutionize policy. Employment exchanges were renamed job centres, were shorn of their duties in benefit administration and were sited in new, attractive premises on major high streets and shopping centres. By 1977, government placements had risen by 30 per cent. On the training front, state grants became available for courses and programmes which helped reduce skill shortages in key sectors. What was so novel about the new policy in general, and the Training Opportunities Programme (TOPs) in particular, was that it did not aim simply at the unemployed, but sought to tackle the whole problem of labour market restructuring with a view to anticipating future demands. Training and retraining in the course of a working life were essential if labour market deficiencies were not to slow down the pace of change.

What initially appeared to be a revolution in the making was subsequently readapted to cope with the unemployment crisis of the 1970s and 1980s. This is not the place to rehearse the fate of all the MSC schemes set up during this time. It is worth noting, however, that they switched from being a strategy to cope with labour market problems in general to a solution for the youth unemployment crisis in particular. The idea of government playing a major part in all retraining and redeployment went by the board as state agencies reverted to their residual role. TOPs was scrapped and the job centres, like the employment exchanges before them, became solely used by employers for low-grade and ill-paid vacancies which they found hard to fill by other means. Unemployed school leavers were the MSC's chief client group by the late 1970s, under the Youth Opportunities Programme (renamed the Youth Training Scheme in 1982 and extended from one year to two). The Community Programme in the early 1980s proved the direct descendant of earlier public works schemes. In 1987 this was scrapped in favour of the Job Training Scheme, which was renamed Employment Training in 1988. CP, JTS and ET are all aimed at the long-term unemployed, but make no secret of the fact that their main target is the under-twenty-five age group. The main change of policy in the 1980s has been in the privatization of such initiatives. While interwar governments used educational establishments, voluntary agencies and local authorities as the means to restore work discipline, the Thatcher administration has fostered the reintroduction of pauper apprenticeships, providing public money to the private commercial sector in return for the services of young people who would otherwise be totally dependent on the state.

In recent years, the allowances given to the new army of 'trainees' have been progressively reduced. YTS recruits at least get an allowance; they are not permitted to claim state benefits anyway. And the chief difference between JTS and ET lies in the amount the unemployed earn on such projects, which was cut back to equal benefit payments plus a supplement of £10 in 1988. The trouble with 'workfare' stems from precisely this point: workers on specific projects find their pay determined not by the job, but by their varying personal circumstances. As with poor law apprentices, there is no incentive to work hard – or, indeed, at all. Both on JTS and ET, the unemployed are voting with their feet. The drop-out rate has been very high, largely because working for £10 a week is considered to be an insult, but also because the scheme is catering for a group now in their mid-twenties, who left school as the recession struck, who have been shifted from one scheme to another and who have never had the chance of a 'real' job.

Over the last decade, YOP, YTS, CP, JTS and all the rest have been heavily criticized either for providing no training at all, or more recently for sponsoring work experience of a semi-skilled nature in service sector jobs where there are already a surfeit of experienced people. The original purpose of MSC training, to foster skills in areas of shortage, notably computing and associated 'high technology' skills, has been forgotten. Today's trainees are hair-dressers' assistants, check-out personnel, typists and keyboard operators, garage forecourt attendants (if they are lucky): shelf stockers and floor sweepers (if they are not). ET was introduced, like YTS before it, to raise the quality of training available under a previous scheme aimed specifically at the long-term unemployed. In both cases, employers are supposed to release trainees for a given period in order to enable them to get a modicum of formal training over and above the acquisition of 'work experience'. In neither case have the 'qualifications' available achieved much value in the market-place. Those failing to secure a permanent position with their original employer are not particularly attractive to others; as usual, business and industry are generally indifferent to state training or those who have completed state schemes. There is little reason for them to suspect they are missing out on something. Thanks to government parsimony in funding these initiatives, those involved in providing the training are frequently completely unqua-lified themselves.

Conclusions

In an era of high unemployment, political priorities have abandoned long-term manpower strategies in favour of measures to massage the statistics and minimize the damage unemployment inflicts on the public purse. This latter-day pauper apprenticeship system – this time managed on a national scale – is still vulnerable to exactly the same criticisms as those levelled at it nearly 200 years ago. The quality of training is still questionable, the application of the system highly varied and open to abuse. The real object of the exercise still appears to be to save public money. State manpower policy has deteriorated into a residual rescue service which might reduce the chances of a particular claimant becoming permanently dependent on state support and might serve to drive down wages. It does, however, involve the state in the public subsidy of private enterprise in a manner quite contrary to the principles Margaret Thatcher and her administration once claimed to support. In this respect at least, Thatcherite policy has not conformed to 'Victorian values.'

Another recent development, reminiscent of the interwar years, has been the emphasis given to encouraging the jobless to move to areas of greater prosperity in search of work. Thanks to the recent expansion in home ownership, new structural constraints are impeding progress in this direction. Differentials in the cost of living make it hard for the unemployed to move to more expensive areas. However, the consequences of such a policy are again being reflected in terms of the damage done to future prosperity not only by leaving depressed areas to fend as best they can, but also by congestion in the south-east. The Barlow Report on the distribution of the industrial population, published in 1940, was a damning indictment of the results of allowing the market free rein in the location of business, industry and housing. Urban sprawl, rising land prices and traffic congestion, as well as the less visible costs in terms of the toll taken by long-distance commuting, were threatening the prosperous areas in the late 1930s as much as they are today. Barlow's solution lay in the extension of central controls and planning regulations, as much to help the congested areas as the deserted depressed regions. It is a document that makes instructive reading today.

State employment and training policies have long been torn between conflicting objectives: the desire to reintegrate the disadvantaged (to save public money) and the need to promote more efficient industrial performance. These requirements are not easily reconciled. Far from promoting efficiency by removing some from the labour market altogether, as Beveridge advocated before the First World War, official placement agencies have always been supposed to also help those that the market rejects. The dilemma has been reinforced in recent years by the creation of statutory safeguards to protect the rights of underprivileged groups in the labour market, notably racial minorities and women. Of course it can be argued that sexual and racial discrimination displays pure, irrational prejudice on the part of many employers. While this may be true, it is beside the point. For the more employers believe that the state service will fob them off with workers they do not want, the less likely they are to trust the system or to use it. They will not support initiatives to further state training programmes; they will shun workers who have completed state schemes. Any attempt by government to force the issue raises questions of managerial prerogative and invites invidious comparisons between state-run and free market economies. Britain's political environment does not permit such a solution.

Overall, Britain's twentieth-century manpower and employment policies have been singularly ineffective in comparison with other countries. This is probably due to the nature of industrial development, which, as this chapter has shown, has meant that the pace of innovation was far from uniform and manpower requirements of industry and business have remained heterogeneous and diffuse. Centralized systems of technical training have, in offering uniform skills, tended not to reflect the immediate requirements of many employers. Hence the preference for 'on the job' training, which has recently permeated government training programmes, a development which naturally means that politicians cannot plan for the future by anticipating skill shortages in growth areas. Coupled with this is a long history of collective bargaining and a *laisser faire* orthodoxy which has encouraged both sides of industry to resist encroachment by the state. Except in times of war, this has meant a reliance on voluntary initiatives which have been largely ignored.

Even Labour governments, with a commitment to the extension of state controls, have been chary of angering the unions by introducing statutory measures and have looked to industry to set its own house in order. Central regulation has proved a clumsy instrument in the question of manpower training. Historical developments indicate that local initiatives were more effective, because they were more flexible and could respond to the collective view of local needs. An awareness of past experience could be salutary to the success of future policy developments in this area.

VI

Comparisons and Conclusions

The Slump: British unemployment policy in comparative perspective

The problem of unemployment has hardly been unique to Britain, although, thanks to land enclosure, early industrialization and the long history of poor relief, the issue assumed political significance earlier in this country than it did elsewhere. In some parts of the globe, the United States and Russia, for example, it was labour dearth rather than labour surplus that periodically posed the biggest challenge to regional economic development. However, by the early twentieth century at least, most major European cities and manufacturing centres were suffering the consequences of cyclical booms and slumps in trade and municipal authorities were taking an active interest in potential remedies for the problem of unemployment in its many and various forms. From the late nineteenth century, the Board of Trade used British consular services to glean information about how the problem was being tackled abroad and, in similar vein, the *Labour Gazette* commanded a wide circulation overseas as other countries became interested in British unemployment policies and their effects. Then as now, public policy-makers were well informed about alternative ways of dealing with the consequences of commercial recession.

As in Britain, the earliest European initiatives to tackle unemployment developed at the municipal level and, until the First World War at least, relatively few countries had developed national policies in this area. By and large, local authorities built on existing private arrangements, providing subventions and encouragement for specialized labour bureaux in Belgium, Germany and France, which had been established by local employers' associations, or by trade unions or by co-operative ventures between the two. Similarly, under the 'Ghent' system (so called after one of the first towns to initiate the scheme in 1901), public grants were supplied to trade unions' and mutual insurance funds which offered unemployment benefits to subscribers. Such subsidies did not come without strings; they were usually conditional on unions extending coverage beyond their normal membership. Even so, these schemes tended to exclude the poorest and most vulnerable, who could not afford to keep up the premiums. Nonetheless, voluntary insurance was popular and was widespread in France, Northern Italy, the low countries and Germany. It provided the foundations of the first national insurance policies in Denmark and Norway in the early twentieth century, where the national government added its own subvention to local funds. The British unemployment insurance scheme in 1911 was unique because it was the first system of compulsory coverage, albeit confined to a limited number of trades.

As employment policies and conditions attached to unemployment relief were structured to suit local circumstances, and as local circumstances varied so widely, comparisons of state policy are invidious before the First World War. The differences in approach only became explicit when national government superseded municipal authority in the determination of policy. In the 1930s, following the Wall Street crash and the subsequent collapse of world trade, comparative assessment becomes that much easier, for no industrialized country remained unaffected by the Slump. In 1928, roughly 10 million people were unemployed worldwide; at the depth of the depression this figure tripled. The scale of the disaster forced a response even from those national governments that had hitherto claimed that labour market regulation was no concern of the state. The impact of the Slump varied considerably – among countries as well as between trades – and its effects were superimposed on very different existing conditions. Unemployment in the 1920s had been relatively low in the United States and France; indeed, the latter country had made extensive use of immigrant labour to make good its labour shortages. In Germany, unemployment had fluctuated wildly between 2 and 18 per cent while in Sweden and Britain, numbers out of work had remained persistently high. Only Britain, however, experienced structural, highly regional unemployment due to overcapacity in her key export trades.

During the Slump, there is little doubt that Germany suffered worst of all. There is no uniform set of data by which trends can be established and international comparisons made. However, official statistics showed that unemployment in Germany peaked just short of 44 per cent of the manual workforce (a figure which has to be reduced to apply to the whole working population). In the United States, unemployment was estimated to have peaked at 25 per cent of the total workforce and in Sweden at slightly less than this. In Britain, as already noted, 22 per cent of insured workers were unemployed in 1933, a figure that falls to 17 per cent when estimating for the working population as a whole. Nor were the industrialized countries the only ones to suffer. The Slump reduced world demand for primary products and thus the recession was transferred to economies chiefly reliant on such exports. In Australia, unemployment reached an estimated 28 per cent in 1932.

In Europe, with the possible exception of Italy, agriculture was less adversely affected than industry. Workers in mining, building, engineering, shipbuilding and metal-work suffered very badly; in Germany, it is hard to find any sector of the economy where unemployment did not rise above 20 per cent in 1932. There, the consequent widespread sense of insecurity, especially among small firms, shopkeepers and artisans, whose businesses were badly hit by falling demand, did much to strengthen the appeal of authoritarian solutions to what appeared to contemporaries to be a miserable economic mess. For the first time skilled workers in depressed trades found themselves out of work alongside their unskilled colleagues. This did much to alter hitherto prevalent popular assumptions about unemployment being the consequence of personal inadequacy and thus strengthened demands for direct state action to deal with the situation. Only in Italy and the USSR did the state already possess the requisite powers to regulate directly both the supply of and demand for labour. In general, the severity of the Slump rocked popular faith in the merits of minimal government and the capacity of the free market to cope with the crisis. This change was reflected particularly in the introduction of Franklin Roosevelt's New Deal programme in the United States, in the election of the social democrats in Sweden in 1932, and in the final triumph of the Nazi Party at the polls in the following year. In France, where high unemployment took longer to emerge, a popular front government was duly elected in 1936 to help confront the problem and to act as a bulwark against fascism. Of all the major industrial countries, only the British electorate remained loyal to classical economic precepts, supporting a National government which retained traditional commitment to public expenditure cuts and minimal state intervention.

This is not to argue that there was no change of policy in Britain in the early 1930s. In common with major trading nations all over the globe, the British government introduced economic incentives designed to promote industrial revival and restore trade. Currencies were devalued, interest rates reduced, tariffs installed to protect home industry (thereby threatening the very trade that all countries wished to promote) and a wide variety of state grants were made available to private enterprise in order to revive production, restore employment and encourage exports. Unlike other governments, however, British policies, some of which were continued from the 1920s, remained confined to indirect intervention to aid recovery. As such initiatives belong essentially to the realm of economic policy, they need not concern us here.[1] What is more pertinent is to contrast the British experience with what occurred elsewhere.

In a variety of countries, policies were developed to create work and to reduce the competition for it by removing particular groups from the labour market. Private industry received public subsidies to extend business, take on extra hands, rotate jobs and share work in various ways. Many governments funded relief work, particularly in agricultural areas, and promoted land settlement schemes. Germany pioneered the first national system of labour camps for unemployed youth. This example was imitated in the United States, Canada, Austria, New Zealand and Scandinavia. In these countries attendance was voluntary, albeit that strong financial incentives existed to encourage recruitment. Public authorities tended to give priority to older workers with families to support when allocating available jobs. The young became prime candidates for transfer into agricultural work or for a spell in a labour camp. This last was less concerned with forced labour as such and more with the preservation of physical and mental fitness in order to counteract the 'demoralization' widely recognized as a direct consequence of prolonged idleness. At the same time, a variety of official pressures were put on women, particularly married women, to remove themselves from the workforce – an area of policy particularly well developed in Germany.

We should not understand this extension of public policy as a sudden, worldwide conversion of politicians to the merits of the demand management strategies advocated by J. M. Keynes. With the exception of Sweden, most government policies continued to bear the hallmark of classical economic orthodoxy. Work incentives were maintained, wages were encouraged to fall. Many official subsidies to industry took the form of loans, to be repaid in better times. State programmes were explained as emergency measures to cope with an unprecedented crisis, not as a permanent extension of official powers. The Keynesian revolution, in short, was the product of the 1940s and the Second World War: informed by the experience of the Slump, but not arising out of it.

In order to appreciate the scope of these initiatives, it is necessary to look at them in a little more detail. Before the US presidential election of 1932, which resulted in his defeat, Herbert Hoover had already offered federal aid to state governments to fund contracyclical public works. Under Franklin Roosevelt's renowned New Deal, this policy was extended and developed. In 1933, about a quarter of a million Americans were employed on these schemes; by June the following year, this figure had reached 600,000, with a further half million taken on in associated industries and local services. The Civil Works Administration (CWA) in 1933–4 employed more than 4 million people on various projects of local improvement: building schools, airports, roads, playgrounds, clearing slums, providing sewers, gas and electricity. The succeeding Works Progress Administration (WPA) took over where the CWA left off. It ran until 1943 and employed some 8.5 million people on similar projects, while also devising special programmes for unemployed actors, authors, journalists and craftsmen. Even so, relief played a more significant role than work under the New Deal. Over and above state-sponsored employment, the Federal Emergency Relief Administration gave the unemployed cash, food and clothing. In the winter of 1934, about 20 million people were dependent on such 'doles'. At the same time, the federal government cut hours for work of its own employees, while encouraging similar action (and other work-sharing systems) in the private sector.

Nazi policy in Germany, while combining direct relief with public employment programmes in a similar fashion, managed to give greater priority to the provision of work than the New Deal ever did. The Nazis, untroubled by American beliefs in the freedom of the individual, injected a degree of compulsion into their labour market policies which was never feasible on the other side of the Atlantic. Hence Hitler's government was able to intervene more forcefully on the question of labour supply. Still, the backbone of the campaign was a huge public works programme, which produced autobahnen, replenished housing stock, repaired and extended railway systems and led to the construction of those massive public buildings and stadia beloved of Albert Speer which characterized the architecture of the Third Reich. The drive for agricultural self-sufficiency, visible in Germany before the First World War and extended after it, was also central to Nazi policy. Subsidies were provided for farms willing to take on more workers. By the end of 1934, 67,000 farms had been created and 117,000 had been extended, notably in East Prussia. State-sponsored 'substitute' employment peaked in 1934 at over a million jobs. At the same time, the Nazis promoted the foundation of industrial cartels, designed to set production targets and to determine wages and prices, while breaking trade union resistance to reductions in take-home pay. Winter dismissals were officially discouraged, work rotation schemes and reduced working hours were promoted, with generous state grants available to employers prepared to co-operate in official schemes.

Tackling the problems of labour supply was made easier by the fact that the unemployed were compelled to take any job offered, whatever the wages or location. This regulation was actually not a Nazi innovation, but originated in legislation passed after the First World War which had rarely been enforced. While the young and single were transferred into agriculture or the labour camps, new restrictions on labour mobility were introduced, to prevent migration to overcrowded towns. Educational requirements for skilled work were reduced and vocational training was extended to handle over half a million recruits a year. One of the main aims of early Nazi manpower policy was to ensure the removal of women from the labour market. In the 1920s, female participation rates had risen and now the state took steps to reverse this trend. Opportunities for women to enter university or train for the professions were restricted to a tiny minority. In 1934, a marriage loans scheme was introduced, providing grants for those who elected to leave paid employment, grants whose repayments were progressively reduced according to the number of children the couple produced. Family allowances were also offered on the birth of children and mothers of large families were accorded particular honour by the state. At the same time, employers were officially encouraged to rid themselves of married women employees. Massive propaganda on the virtues of female domesticity reinforced these developments. Women's patriotic duty lay in their dedication to 'Kinder, Kirche und Küche'. As a result of these combined factors, women left the labour market in droves, a development which was to produce problems in later years when labour shortages threatened the viability of the German war economy.

The hallmark of Nazi policy was its success. Unemployment levels fell remarkably quickly, aided, admittedly, by the government's exclusion of particular 'categories' of workers from the official statistics. Even so, by 1936 labour shortage had replaced labour surplus as the principal manpower problem, well before the German economy had been fully converted to a wartime basis. Hitler's stated objective of achieving 'full employment' was met in under three years. In Germany, public policy was helped by the revival of business confidence that strong government brought in its wake. However, we must not forget the high price paid by German workers for the eradication of unemployment in terms of falling wages and the loss of those political and civil liberties taken for granted in western industrial democracies. Nonetheless, the New Deal never managed to match the Nazi achievement. Full employment in the United States was reached only as rearmament revived levels of labour demand on the eve of the Second World War.

The Swedish response to the Slump presents a different picture.

Here, state intervention was premissed on ideas about demand management. Underconsumption was seen as the root cause of unemployment and a positive employment policy presented the only solution. This early acceptance of Keynesian principles (the Swedish Social Democrats developed their theories before Keynes himself) meant that state regulation of the economy was not justified simply as a temporary emergency measure to counteract natural disaster, as was the case in the United States. Rather the Social Democrats were elected in 1932 on a programme designed to extend state powers permanently in order to guarantee full employment: a commitment maintained by both this and later Swedish governments. In 1933–5, deficit finance was accepted as public expenditure more than doubled in order to stimulate demand. State loans for public works were administered through a National Employment Commission, which gave priority to non-profit-making enterprises able to continue operating through the harsh Swedish winter. Wages were set at about the level of the lowest unskilled worker, but were largely paid by the piece, thereby encouraging individual effort. Redeployment became closely attached to the provision of training. In order to encourage mobility further, the state subsidized both housing and travel costs. The Swedish system tended not to give work to the unemployed in their own communities, but used state employment schemes to foster labour market flexibility and occupational mobility, thereby promoting the restructuring of the economy.

The United States, Germany and Sweden provided the most extensive and co-ordinated national programmes to counteract the consequences of the Slump. They were not, however, entirely exceptional. In Italy, where Mussolini's government had established corporate structures to facilitate state direction of economic development, positive measures were also adopted to counteract recession in industry and agriculture. Indeed, the Italian land resettlement programmes were as advanced as their German counterparts. Other initiatives, although on a more localized scale, were undertaken in Holland and Belgium. In France, both the scale of the problem and official responses to it were much less visible. Rising unemployment caused the expulsion of the foreign immigrants recruited the previous decade and much urban unemployment was absorbed by workers returning to their families in agricultural districts whenever possible. In Britain, the unemployment crisis was met with a campaign of retrenchment. While other nations extended public works and public aid to help the victims of the recession, the British government responded by taking steps to reduce public liability and to contain levels of public expenditure. Commercial enterprise and charitable endeavour, shored up by government encouragement and a very limited amount of financial support, were to prove the main agencies for dealing with the problem. While happy to take measures to stimulate economic recovery in the long term, the British government proved singularly loath to do anything specifically for the unemployed, even on an emergency basis. As a result, unemployment lingered in the depressed areas, only to be mopped up by rearmament and the Second World War.

In comparison with other leading industrial nations, the British response to the Slump appears to be one of studied inactivity. Why this was so merits explanation. Some historians have maintained that high levels of unemployment in the 1920s accustomed both public and politicians to the crisis conditions of the following decade, which were experienced much more sharply in Germany and America. However, this does not help explain why the Swedish response differed so markedly from the British, when both countries had large numbers out of work before the Slump occurred. More plausibly, Britain did not have the capacity for self-sufficiency found in Germany and the United States, was more reliant on trade to restore prosperity and British governments were therefore always more reluctant to intervene in any way that might prejudice British interests in financial or commercial markets abroad. However, Britain did have overseas colonies; a system of imperial preference allowing the Empire to develop as a self-sufficient market was a distinct possibility and one strongly advocated by Oswald Mosley both within the Labour Party and subsequently within the British Union of Fascists. This policy simply failed to attract sufficient popular support. As an alternative explanation, we could look to the tradition of minimal state intervention, particularly strong in the heyday of industrialization, which caused both electorate and politicians to associate economic growth and prosperity with the ethos of *laisser faire*. This historical framework was very different from that of Germany, which lacked any strong liberal tradition and where industrialization had developed under the aegis of a paternalist state. However, the United States, with an equally strong cultural faith in the merits of individualism and free enterprise, adopted much more extensive measures to help the unemployed than those found in Britain.

Instead, as in 1983, the British electorate turned its back on political platforms promoting state intervention in response to the unemployment crisis. Although the explanations offered above evidently play some part in explaining this paradox, a major contributor to the climate of political acquiescence was the British system of state benefits. This, whatever its other shortcomings, gave the unemployed a modicum of financial support which was simply not available elsewhere. When the crisis struck, about 38 million of the world's workers were covered by compulsory unemployment insurance. Of these, 31 million were in Britain and Germany, the balance belonging largely to an Italian scheme for industrial workers. As in Britain, the sheer numbers out of work threw the German scheme into chaos. Unlike Britain, the last Weimar governments were unable to patch together a comprehensive system which could tide the unemployed over into better times; there were too many making claims on state funds. Between 1930 and 1932, contributions to the German scheme were repeatedly raised while benefits fell by 23 per cent: a process complicated by the fact that the German scheme, unlike the British, involved earnings-related benefits and contributions. A comprehensive means test was introduced from the seventh week of unemployment (as opposed to the twenty-seventh week in Britain) in a vain attempt to restore the German scheme to solvency while maintaining political credibility. Literally millions of workers were thus thrown back on to stringent local public assistance and emergency schemes of 'Winterhilfe'. Local authorities were even less able to prevent destitution and hunger, factors stimulating the social and political discord and violence which helped create a climate conducive to fascism.

State-sponsored voluntary insurance, which covered around 4 million European workers in 1930, failed to give help to those worst hit by the Slump. Even within their limited capacity, the schemes did not fare well. Contributory income slumped as claims soared; both local and national governments were forced to shore up funds to prevent total collapse. The extension of official liability was accompanied by stricter state regulation and control; the old Ghent system lost its flexibility and became more uniform in coverage. This was notably true in Denmark, whose national government had been subsidizing local funds since 1908. In France, local authorities were responsible for official contributions to the 'fonds de chomage'; many collapsed as a result of the strain. In 1934, only 737 funds (covering 2,087 out of 37,000 communes) were still extant. And in the United States, no federal system of unemployment relief existed at all. Where they existed, a tiny minority of unemployed Americans might receive help from their firm, their trade union, from charity or from state relief. Similarly, in Sweden in the 1920s, most workers relied on union-based schemes of unemployment benefits, while public relief operated on deterrent principles similar to the British poor law.

With the exception of Britain, social security reform followed in the wake of state schemes of job creation and new manpower initiatives. In Sweden, Germany and the United States, the introduction (or revival) of unemployment insurance was set firmly within the context of broader employment initiatives and, unlike Britain, was not understood as an alternative to them. In Germany, a redefined insurance scheme became a powerful tool for labour market management, with a complex structure of benefit rights regulated according to the needs of the Nazi economy. Elsewhere, the question of relief remained in the background of unemployment policy. Under the Social Security Act 1935, the Roosevelt administration introduced unemployment and old age benefits, but handed all initiative in the formulation and implementation of the legislation back to the individual states, thereby promoting a heterogeneous and idiosyncratic system of unemployment relief across the United States as a whole. In Sweden, the system of state-sponsored unemployment insurance introduced in 1934 was voluntary. Operating on the Danish model, it allowed public funds to be provided for trade union schemes in return for an official voice in how these funds were spent. In the event, the subsidies were too small, and the attractions of maintaining independence too great, to encourage widespread co-operation. By the outbreak of the Second World War, only 20 per cent of trade union members were covered by the state scheme – and Sweden possessed the most unionized workforce in the world. The majority preferred union benefits adapted to their employment and circumstances and independent of legal regulation.

The 1930s thus stimulated a breakthrough in international unemployment policy, albeit one that barely touched Britain. In measures to create jobs, encourage industry, extend official powers in the training and redeployment of manpower, we can see how governments responded positively to the crisis, although in only one case (Sweden) were new policies founded on quasi-Keynesian principles. The momentum established by the Slump was consolidated in the aftermath of the Second World War, when governments all around the world made public commitments to full employment. Keynesian theory now showed how state intervention in economic affairs was not merely permissable but positively essential to the promotion of general prosperity. Keynes's prescriptions were not confined to internal economic, monetary and fiscal policies. The General Agreement on Tariffs and Trade (GATT) was established to outlaw protection, which had so reduced the volume of world trade before the war. The International Monetary Fund (IMF) was created to prevent any future international financial crisis precipitating another commercial collapse. For a full generation after the fall of Hitler's Germany, international and national economic policies in the western industrial economies aimed to ensure that the unemployment of the 1930s, with its associations of human misery, political extremism and subsequent world war, could never return.

All this now seems to be history. Mass unemployment again became an international problem in the early 1980s. This time the crisis was less sudden and did not stimulate the extreme political responses characteristic of the 1930s. Nearly a century later, the political heirs of the *laisser faire* liberals, the so-called 'new right', have advocated what they claim are new policies to deal with the problem, which signal a return to neo-classical economic precepts. Individual incentive is to be restored by cutting taxation, levels of public expenditure and support for the clients of state welfare – particularly the unemployed themselves. There has been a general loss of faith in government as an agency for social amelioration;

private enterprise and a free labour market are claimed to be the sole mechanisms which can generate the return of prosperity. However, political pressures have limited the influence of monetarist theory as a blueprint for public policy. Behind the rhetoric of economic liberalism, barriers have been erected to protect domestic industry from overseas competition. Rising unemployment has seen the return of aid to industry, the development of training, relief work and various job subsidies. The small scale of these initiatives, however, betrays their intent. In the early 1980s, governments contrived to 'muddle through', using a variety of traditional palliatives less to restructure and revitalize economies than to reduce the official level of unemployment at minimal cost to the public purse. Even the Swedes, pioneers in the field of state planning, resorted to emergency assistance for industries in trouble with the short-term aim of saving jobs. The most depressing aspect of unemployment in the 1980s is that public policy seems to be so short on new ideas.

Conclusions

The history of the 1930s is salutary; the British government's response differed markedly from that of the other main industrial powers. In line with its own traditions and in contrast to other countries, Britain's policy focused on the question of unemployment relief, to the exclusion of more or less everything else. Policy for the unemployed still betrayed the political and cultural heritage of the nineteenth century – that of the poor law and the *laisser faire* orthodoxy that underpinned it. The administration of relief for the able-bodied destitute was transferred from local to national government. Unlike most other countries, the British government sought to reduce public expenditure on unemployment. Means tests were extended, local job creation was abandoned. Reformers claimed that removing policy from the vagaries of local administration promoted uniformity and, therefore, social justice. This assertion seems dubious. The establishment of a national policy fostered a certain rigidity of practice: central regulation could not respond to the variations in labour management that characterized different industries and different regions. In short, the imposition of uniform rules on heterogeneous industrial practices could not promote social justice; if anything, it threatened to do quite the opposite.

It is doubtful whether this initiative succeeded in eliminating variations in local practice during the 1930s. After the Second World War, thanks to full employment and the rise of trade union bargaining power, employment became more regular. It remained so for the next forty years, long enough to become regarded as 'normal'. The recent expansion of self-employment, part-time work and short-term contracts seems to indicate a return to earlier patterns. This should cause us again to question the utility of a single set of criteria in identifying (and helping) the unemployed. The issue of uniformity aside, recent developments in the administration of unemployment relief have revived old assumptions and principles, serving to remind us of the importance of past precedent in shaping public policy in this area. As in the 1930s, politicians in the 1980s have repeatedly asserted the need to promote flexible (meaning downwardly flexible) wage rates, to encourage the search for jobs, to restore work incentives by reducing both access to and the value of state benefits, and to contain levels of public expenditure by increasing central control over local government. The law has long required the state to relieve the destitute. This, combined with the tradition of *laisser faire*, has produced a peculiarly British form of unemployment policy, which allows social security a dominant role in shaping the labour market and determining access to it. Hence this country played a pioneering role in the development of national insurance, while generally failing to promote any positive policies on training, redeployment or industrial restructuring.

There are other ways in which we can see that the nineteenth century has left its mark. The preference of the British for systems of social insurance which confer benefits 'as of right', and their dislike of means tests owes much to the stigma and disgrace associated with poor relief. This stands in marked contrast, for example, to the experience of Australia, which never had a poor law, where compulsory contributions have always been highly unpopular, and where liberal means tests have been generally acceptable. The British dislike of means testing has been reflected in a long history of low take-up of many state benefits. The recently established Social

Fund is not popular. Many claimants prefer to raise loans on the commercial market, with its horrendous rates of interest: only the desperate resort to the state. Benefit cuts have fostered violence in social security offices, while encouraging the unemployed to buck the system whenever possible, thereby increasing the cost of policing administration. Recent attempts to force claimants into unpleasant, low-paid work by tightening access to benefits are no replacement for effective manpower policies, raising investment in human capital to promote future prosperity.

In some respects, efforts to keep the working classes independent of state support have succeeded, while fostering forms of self-help that have not always been welcomed by free market economists. The demand for waged work has grown apace. In the sphere of industrial relations, trade unions allied themselves with employers in resisting the encroachments of the state and in defending the sphere of free collective bargaining. In this respect, organized labour sought to strengthen its hold over the provision of work and access to jobs. Indeed, the consequences of the 1930s and the Slump were made manifest in the 1950s and 1960s, when union men from the executive to the shop floor fought to preserve obsolete manning levels, to maintain outdated forms of job demarcation, to resist the encroachment of new technology and generally to legitimize 'restrictive practices'. Strategies to protect jobs were motivated by the fear that depression would return and force union members back into the clutches of the 'means test man'. Hence, far from encouraging a flexible labour market, as Chadwick and Nassau Senior had argued it would, a deterrent system of unemployment relief produced such fears of unemployment as to make industrial labour fight to preserve the very labour market rigidities that an efficient manpower policy would have removed. The structure of British trade unionism has not helped. Having evolved over time to protect the interests of particular trades or groups of skilled men, unions have generally been hostile to strategies designed to restructure whole industries, whether initiated by government or employers. In Sweden, by contrast, industrial unionism was established before the First World War and this form of labour representation was able to accommodate national employment policies when these were introduced in the 1930s. In Britain, however, it is not possible to analyse labour market policy without appreciating how industrial relations has influenced its nature and limited its scope.

In the interface between public policy and industrial practice, government initiatives have proved notoriously weak. Employment policies in Britain have been remarkable for their singular lack of success. In part, this has stemmed from faith in a free labour market and the persistent belief that industry knows best how to set its house in order – a view promoted assiduously by industry itself. Even in the heyday of state management of the economy after the Second World War, it is evident that neither Westminister nor Whitehall had much idea about what manpower policy or manpower planning might entail once wartime controls were abolished. This allowed industrial representatives on the myriad of advisory councils and committees set up inside major government departments to defend the traditional borderline between public policy and private management. Questions of training, recruitment and redeployment were kept firmly within the province of free collective bargaining. Hence, in the decades following the end of the war, the government relied solely on fiscal and monetary policy to regulate levels of labour demand while, elsewhere in Europe, greater attention was paid to questions of industrial policy and manpower planning. Britain's political culture thus prevented the development of more sophisticated strategies for tackling the problems of industrial decline.

The extension of state-sponsored training programmes under the aegis of the MSC was supposed to initiate a break with the past, allowing government more say in shaping the labour market according to the needs of the future. However, the extensive schemes of state-sponsored industrial and technical training found in Germany are not reproduced in the projects created under YTS or ET. The emphasis currently placed on employer-based work experience, with only a few weeks' formal training loosely attached, is more reminiscent of the eighteenth-century system of pauper apprenticeships than of a new, modern training policy for the post-industrial age. The current crisis has stimulated a return to traditional palliatives, not a radical departure from them. The original objective of the MSC, to create a comprehensive manpower policy, has gone by the board. Policy on training and redeployment has reverted to a residual role, concentrating solely on young people immediately surplus to market requirements rather than on the workforce as a whole. For the rest, the governments of the 1980s have looked to private employers to invest more in their own training programmes, arguing that the market knows best what skills it requires in the future and therefore the market will invest more wisely than government possibly can.

The results have been less than encouraging. Employer-based training in the 1980s has been patchy and has concentrated over-whelmingly on firm-specific skills, of limited utility in the promotion of general industrial growth. Many firms still rely on high salaries and auxiliary benefits to attract ready-trained personnel from elsewhere; they are reluctant to train for their own needs. What is more alarming is the way in which state sponsorship of higher education has also been restricted. Britain has a lower proportion of sixteen- and seventeen-year-olds in full-time education than its main industrial rivals. As the increasing pace of technological change demands extensive retraining programmes to update skills, the general standard of education among the working population ought to rise in order to endow as many as possible with the ability to adopt and utilize new techniques. To compete, the British government must invest large amounts of money in education and training, if only to achieve the standards reached elsewhere in western Europe. In 1884, the Samuelson Commission concluded that the neglect of education and training by the state in Britain was one of the key factors in losing ground to industrial competitors. After a century of delay and with the advent of the Single European Market imminent, the attainment of international standards in vocational and higher education is now an urgent matter.

One way of tackling the unemployment issue in the 1980s has been to redefine its scope: to exclude the 'unemployable' and to identify the 'real' unemployed. The construction of the problem has hardly remained consistent over time. On the contrary, the answer to the question 'who counts as unemployed?' has proved highly responsive to social and political pressures. The first legal definition of unemployment, drawn up in 1911, reflected labour management strategies found in trades covered by the new unemployment insurance scheme. The general notion of unemployment that had emerged at the end of the nineteenth century had been a good deal less precise. It was a term applied to that group of potential destitutes whose temporary lack of income could not be ascribed to age, infirmity, industrial dispute, criminal disposition or personal disinclination to work regular hours. However, as observers discovered, labour market disorganization prevented the easy identification of such a group. As a result, early unemployment debates were shot through with references to decasualization and labour market reform in an attempt to make reality conform to theory. The concept of unemployment was fashioned by the process of political debate, a debate informed in part by the desire to raise standards of industrial efficiency, in part by the application of social scientific research to labour market problems, and in part by the definitions of unemployment used in those trades where labour was discharged when times were hard. In all these areas, the unemployed were identified not merely by their physical capacity for work, but by their attitude towards it. The feckless, the lazy, the drunken did not 'count' as unemployed. Policy developed to distinguish the regular worker from the 'residuum': to support the former in hard times, but to expel the latter from the labour market altogether. Opinion differed over precisely where this line should be drawn; the general aim was to offer members of each group treatment appropriate to their condition.

In this way, a national identity of the 'unemployed' came into being. Normative, uniform definitions, devised by a relatively small political élite, were superimposed on a diverse range of established industrial practices, evidently with a view to their reformation. Whatever the objective, this degree of homogeneity may have made for administrative simplicity and convenience, but it did not lead to social justice. In its early years, the system bred resistance. In the aftermath of the First World War, a more powerful labour movement came to challenge earlier preconceptions and to force their reconsideration. Local authorities charged with poor relief and employers liable to national insurance contributions also held strong views about the identification of the 'unemployed' within the group of generally impoverished. In the course of the interwar period, the concept of unemployment was uprooted from its foundations in social scientific discourse and thrown open to the vagaries of political debate and compromise. As a result, the term was adapted to embrace groups it had originally been designed to exclude, the 'long-term' unemployed and certain groups of casual and short-time workers being cases in point.

The well-organized sectors of the labour force, particularly those in the old staple export trades, did quite well out of this process. On the docks, casual labourers (who had, in Edwardian times, epitomized the 'residuum' and its attendant problems) now claimed state benefits to supplement irregular earnings. More generally, workers stuck in declining industries in the depressed areas – coal-mining, shipbuilding, engineering – managed to retain their status as 'unemployed' as opposed to 'pauper', although the introduction of the household means test in 1931 for long-term cases made the distinction largely nominal. In contrast, the less politically influential members of the labour force, notably women, found access to state unemployment benefit severely curtailed and ceased to 'count' as part of the problem. History demonstrates how political factors played a central part in shaping contemporary understanding of unemployment and in identifying its victims. This is a continuous process. The recent crisis has stimulated further redefinitions which, broadly speaking, have also served to exclude the less politically volatile from the official statistics: married women, school leavers and volunteers for early retirement being notable examples.

Those excluded from one category of social dependency have tended to find their way into another. Those without work owing to sickness, disability or old age have long been classified separately. Similarly, vagrant casuals have been regarded as a distinct group and policies have been specifically developed to deal with them. Even though both their wandering and their poverty might token their need for work, they are not generally perceived as 'unemployed'. In practice, what we might term the social pathology of joblessness has operated in a fairly idiosyncratic fashion. Considerable overlap exists between the various categories; the classification of applicants has reflected not only advances in medical understanding, but also the prevailing state of the labour market. In the 1940s, manpower shortages resulted not merely in falling levels of unemployment, but also in a markedly lower incidence of vagrancy and long-term sickness. General levels of social dependency fell in response to rising rates of economic activity.

Conversely, high unemployment discourages those in poor health from seeking work. When the labour market is overcrowded, the significance of a minor medical ailment increases, especially in the eyes of the sufferer convinced that it is ruining his chances of a job. While the strain imposed by unemployment may foster physical and mental deterioration, it may also encourage the marginal candidate to alter his registration from 'unemployed' to 'sick', without any change in his state of health necessarily taking place at all. This avoids the social disgrace associated with jobless-ness and is encouraged when higher rates of benefit can be claimed by those registering as sick or disabled rather than unemployed (as was the case in both the 1930s and the 1980s). A glut of labour on the market will also encourage people to 'retire' from work earlier, even though these older workers are much healthier and more capable of work today than ever before. The lowering of retirement age is a time-honoured strategy for coping with industrial recession; this has developed in both formal and informal ways.

The incidence and distribution of unemployment are not the simple product of economic trends. The process of distinguishing the unemployed from the rest of the economically inactive in the adult population has been shaped in part by political debate, in part by industrial and social change. Collective bargaining has played a part in both. Discussion has been influenced by the prevailing economic climate, but has primarily reflected conflicting ideologies about the mechanics of the labour market as well as assumptions about desirable forms of social organization and behaviour. British unemployment figures do not reflect the total numbers out of work; they do not now and they never have. It is unjustifiable to castigate official statistics for failing to show the 'real' extent of unemploy-ment without appreciating that there is no 'real' unemployment. As the analysis here indicates, unemployment is essentially an artificial construct. In some parts of the world, such as Hong Kong, it does not officially exist. Other countries try to avoid the ambiguities imposed by Britain's administrative valuations by using survey questionnaires when compiling their unemployment figures. This does not avoid the problem. Both the current chances of finding a job and changes in personal circumstance will still determine whether or not an individual claims to be seeking work. Over and above this, domestic levels of unemployment in Europe and America have been protected from the worst fluctuations of labour demand by the judicious recruitment – and expulsion – of foreign workers, whose employment status has remained unrecognized by the host country. Britain's geographical position has made this process both more visible and more liable to legal regulation. Whatever the other indignities suffered by recent immigrants from the 'new Commonwealth', minority demands for their forceable repatriation have, to date, fallen on deaf ears.

When subject to scrutiny, the notion of unemployment loses any precise definition. The concept has no absolute scientific status. Once this is accepted, the limitations on the usefulness of a purely statistical definition of the problem, which is the form in which unemployment is usually appraised and discussed, become obvious. An historical perspective also helps demolish one or two myths which are still attached to the unemployment question. First, higher rates of economic growth do not provide an automatic solution to the problem. Quite apart from the debate about whether the development of new industry would raise the overall demand for labour, we must recognize that the unemployed are unlikely to benefit from this process. They live in the 'wrong' places and cannot afford to move to more prosperous areas; they may not possess the requisite skills. More importantly, successful entrepreneurs have long shown a reluctance to employ those cast off by failing industries, preferring instead to recruit new labour market entrants. Hence it is possible for economic growth to generate new jobs without reducing the numbers out of work. In the mid-1980s, this happened: both economic activity rates and unemployment rose at the same time. Historically, the only time that unemployment has been dramatically reduced has been during the two world wars, when the programme of rearmament revived demand for old skills in heavy industry.

We should also question whether a free labour market provides the best solution to the unemployment problem. Supporters of this theory frequently point to late nineteenth-century Britain as an era of social harmony and economic expansion, demonstrating the merits of *laisser faire*. There are several reasons for querying this idealized interpretation. In the first place, it is wrong to assume that the state played no part in regulating the labour market at this time. The apprenticeship laws were formally abolished early in the nineteenth century, but they were replaced by factory legislation in the 1830s which aimed to make manufacturers reject female and child labour in favour of prime age males. Although politicians paid lip-service to the ideology of *laisser faire*, local government at the end of the century was increasingly involved in the provision of local services, the fostering of local enterprise and the regulation of local labour markets by sponsoring labour intensive public projects when rising unemployment threatened social disruption. Official agencies played a part in managing local labour markets and in stimulating the economy. For these reasons, the 'golden age' of the free market – like so many others – appears less golden on closer inspection than we might initially suppose.

Let us, for the sake of argument, assume that the late nineteenth century did witness a decline in official intervention in the labour market. Is it possible to conclude that, left to its own devices, the market performed effectively, eliminating the least productive workers and generating competitive and efficient industrial enterprise? Contemporary opinion, from all sides of the political spectrum and within professional and administrative circles, inclined to the opposite view. The unregulated labour market in major urban centres fostered casualism, sweating, chronic underemployment and, with this, a degree of perpetual poverty which rendered its victims sickly, dispirited and unproductive. The effects of urban degeneration were not confined to the rising costs of the poor law, but spread to threaten the viability of British commerce and the very security of Empire. The first attempts to increase state regulation were not made by socialist radicals, but by the party traditionally associated with the promotion of industrial enterprise, which abandoned its previous faith in the merits of *laisser faire*. There is no evidence here to suggest that labour markets operate more efficiently when government does not intervene.

Nonetheless, faith in the free market has returned to dominate British thinking on the unemployment problem and state policies for the unemployed, which are among the most illiberal in Europe.

Its appeal lies in the elemental simplicity of classical and neo-classical economics. This understands unemployment almost purely in terms of an excess of labour supply over demand, which can be eased by the adjustment of relative labour costs. In the real world, however, unemployment has been constructed in a more complex fashion. Our understanding of the issue has come to accommodate the political demands voiced by organized labour, which interprets the scope of the problem in quite a different way. However, if we accept that unemployment is politically constructed – which seems so obvious as to be a truism – we can also accept that it is responsive to political solutions. If we are prepared to deny that both the problem and its amelioration are solely the product of impersonal and uncontrollable market forces, then we can accept that governments and their agencies are capable of tackling the issue to good effect. All in all, this perspective offers a far more optimistic view than the alternative.

The question remains, of course, of what can be done, short of establishing the sort of regimentation that Hitler introduced into the German labour market in the 1930s. Because unemployment is the obverse of employment, whatever form that takes, it seems that part of the solution lies in tackling the issue of work. Why is full-time employment so important in people's lives? Might steps be taken to make it less important? Both modern technology and the information economy (increasingly significant influences on the job market today) offer an escape from the dictatorship of the regulated full-time working week, itself an anachronism inherited from a past when a large sector of the workforce was attached to mechanized production. The reason that this anachronism is lovingly preserved and protected is partly to do with custom and expectation, but equally to do with the protection and status given by government to full-time workers. They cannot be arbitrarily dismissed, they have a guaranteed income when on holiday or sick, they receive an earnings related pension on retirement. Further, they can raise a mortgage on a house, can command extensive credit with few questions asked, and can afford hire-purchase on more expensive goods. In the upper echelons of the labour market, a secure income is supplemented by subsidized transport, private health care, private school fees and so on. If full-time employment secures such privileges, no wonder there is such pressure on these jobs. One of the primary steps government might take to encourage labour market flexibility lies in realigning work incentives to the benefit of other groups: the growing army of self-employed, part-time workers and casuals. If more irregular patterns of employment are essential to the development of new economic prosperity, then government must accept the need to look again at the penalties incurred by workers who abandon job security and take steps to reduce, even abolish, them.

Of course, historians have no business becoming involved in the future; their area of expertise lies in the past. Prescription should be left to other pundits. However, as this book has demonstrated, the recent appearance of more irregular forms of employment cannot be understood as a 'new' development, but represents (in part) a return to older practices. Past attempts to divide the labour market into two discreet groups – the 'employed' and 'unemployed' – have, for much of this century, ignored large numbers of people whose working lives do not allow them to be placed comfortably in either category. In this respect at least, the years following the Second World War were exceptional. These decades fostered the impression that 'full' employment was normal and that rising rates of joblessness were a deviation from that 'norm'. A longer historical time span tells a different story. When the history of twentieth-century Britain comes to be written, it will point to the similarities between past crises and the present one – similarities which are currently too often overlooked. The 1950s, not the 1980s, will be seen as the 'exceptional' decade. We would all profit greatly by learning from past experience, by understanding how unemployment is constructed by managerial practices specific to particular trades and businesses at particular times, by realizing that little is gained when we superimpose uniform definitions of labour market status on wide variations in employment practice. Otherwise, there is a real risk that public understanding and political debate will become stuck in modes of thought similar, if not identical, to those which have dominated this area of discussion since the days of the industrial revolution.

Notes

Chapter I: The Recent Crisis

1 Unemployment data for the 1930s in this chapter has been drawn from C. H. Feinstein, *Statistical Tables of National Income, Expenditure and Output of the United Kingdom* (Cambridge University Press, 1976), Table 58.
2 Official unemployment figures for the 1980s in this chapter are taken from Central Statistical Office, *Social Trends*, no. 9 (1989), unless otherwise stated.
3 Department of Employment, *Gazette*, August 1989, Table 2.4.
4 Ibid., Tables 2.5, 2.8.
5 Claims to long-term sickness benefits rose by one-third between 1981 and 1985. See *Government Expenditure Plans, 1985–6 to 1987–8*, Cmd. 9428–II.
6 As reported in *The Economist*, 27 November, 1986, p. 68.
7 A more detailed analysis of historical developments in this area is given in Chapter 4.
8 N. Gray (ed.), *The Worst of Times* (Wildwood House, 1985), p. 36.
9 B. Campbell, *Wigan Pier Revisited* (Virago, 1984), p. 179.
10 Ibid., p. 173.

Chapter II: Historical Perspectives

1 Flora Thompson, *Lark Rise to Candleford* (Penguin Books, 1976), pp. 79–80.
2 George Bourne, *Change in the Village* (Duckworth, 1912), p. 133.
3 E. P. Thompson and E. Yeo (eds), *The Unknown Mayhew* (Penguin Books, 1973), p. 471.
4 Robert Tressell, *The Ragged Trousered Philanthropists* (Lawrence & Wishart, 1955), pp. 402–3.
5 E. Rathbone and G. H. Wood, *Report of an Enquiry into the Condition of Dock Labour at the Port of Liverpool* (Liverpool Economic and Statistical Society: Transactions, 1903–4), p. 54.
6 Quoted in M. Neumann, *The Speenhamland County* (Garland, 1982), p. 199.
7 William Cobbett, quoted in E. P. Thompson, *The Making of the English Working Class* (Penguin Books, 1968), p. 836.
8 Richard Oastler, quoted in E. Hopkins, *Social History of the English Working Classes* (Edward Arnold, 1979), p. 93.

9 K. Snell, *Annals of the Labouring Poor* (Cambridge University Press, 1982), p. 133.

10 Quoted in J. Knott, *Popular Opposition to the 1834 Poor Law* (Croom Helm, 1986), p. 232.

Chapter III: Theory and Opinion: The Politics of Unemployment

1 Friedrich Engels, *The Condition of the Working Class in England* (Panther Books, 1969), pp. 113–14.

2 Royal Commission on the Poor Laws, *Appendix*, vol. III (Cd. 4755/1909), p. 35, Q.78153.

3 A. Paterson, *Across the Bridges* (Edward Arnold, 1911), p. 164.

Chapter IV: Redefining Unemployment: The Interwar Years

1 N. Gray (ed.), *The Worst of Times* (Wildwood House, 1985), pp. 164–5.

2 Max Cohen, *I Was One of the Unemployed* (Gollancz, 1945), p. 152.

3 In 1933, the 'reasonable expectation' requirement was watered down and rates of disallowance dropped to around 30,000–40,000 a year (Papers on file PIN 7/158, Public Record Office).

4 Royal Commission on Unemployment Insurance, *Appendices*, Part III (HMSO, 1931), Appendix XXII, Evidence, p. 113.

5 George Orwell, *Collected Essays, Journalism and Letters*, vol. 1 (Penguin Books, 1982), p. 199.

6 To incorporate all who had made twenty-six contributions in two years. This even allowed tramps and itinerant casuals to claim benefit on occasion – even though they were disqualified under the UAB as being of no fixed abode.

Chapter V: State Training and Unemployment Policies

1 *The Times*, 22 March 1938, leading article.

2 Royal Commission on the Poor Laws, *Appendix*, vol. III, (Cd. 4755/1909), p. 167.

3 'Withdrawal of Benefit from Men Refusing to Attend a Training Centre', CP 37(30), 3 February 1930, CAB 24/209, Public Record Office.

4 UAB memo 281, AST 7/314, Public Record Office.

Chapter VI: Comparisons and Conclusions

1 See the companion volume to this one: S. Glynn, *No Alternative? Unemployment in Britain* (Historical Handbooks, Faber and Faber, 1991).

Select Bibliography

The central chapters in this book contain reworked material taken from the author's earlier publications, which are included below.

Alexander, S., Davin, A. and Hostetler, E., 'Labouring Women', *History Workshop Journal*, 8, 1979.

Bakke, E., *The Unemployed Man*, New York, 1933.

Benjamin, D. K. and Kochin, L. A., 'Searching for an Explanation of Unemployment in Interwar Britain', *Journal of Political Economy*, 87, 1979. (Further discussion of this article can be found in *Journal of Political Economy*, 90, 1982.)

Beveridge, W., *Unemployment, a Problem of Industry*, London, 1909 and 1930.

——, *Full Employment in a Free Society*, London, 1944.

Booth, A. and Pack, M., *Employment, Capital and Economic Policy: Great Britain 1918–39*, Oxford, 1985.

Brittan, S., *Second Thoughts on Full Employment Policy*, Chichester, 1975.

Brown, K., *Labour and Unemployment, 1900–1914*, Newton Abbott, 1971.

Burman, S. (ed.), *Fit Work for Women*, London, 1979.

Burnett, J. (ed.), *Useful Toil: Autobiographies of Working People from the 1820s to the 1920s*, London, 1974.

Bythall, D., *The Sweated Trades*, London, 1978.

Cairncross, A., 'The Postwar Years', in Floud and McCloskey.

Coleman, D. C., 'Labour in the English Economy of the Seventeenth Century', *Economic History Review*, 2nd series, VIII, 1956.

Colledge, M. and Bartholomew, R. (eds), *A Study of the Long Term Unemployed*, London, 1980.

Constantine, S., *Unemployment in Britain Between the Wars*, London, 1980.

Crick, B. (ed.), *Unemployment*, London, 1981.

Daniel, W., *A National Survey of the Unemployed*, London, 1974.

——, *The Unemployed Flow*, PSI London, 1981.

Davidson, R., *Whitehall and the Labour Problem in Late Victorian and Edwardian Britain*, London, 1981.

Deacon, A., 'An End to the Means Test? Social Security and the Attlee Government', *Journal of Social Policy*, 11, 1982.

——, *In Search of the Scrounger*, London, 1976.

—— and Bradshaw, J., *Reserved for the Poor*, Oxford, 1983.

—— and Briggs, E., 'The Creation of the Unemployment Assistance Board', *Policy and Politics*, 2, 1974.

Digby, A., *Pauper Palaces*, London, 1979.

——, *The Poor Law in Nineteenth Century England and Wales*, Historical Association, London, 1981.

Disney, R., 'Theorising the Welfare State: the Case of Unemployment Insurance in Britain', *Journal of Social Policy*, 11, 1982.

Disraeli, B., *Sybil, or the Two Nations*, Harmondsworth, 1980 edn.

Doeringer, P. B. and Piore, M. J., *Internal Labor Markets and Manpower Analysis*, Farnborough, 1971.

Eisenberg, D. and Lazarsfeld, P., 'The Psychological Effects of Unemployment', *Psychological Bulletin*, 35, 1933.

Feinstein, C. H., *National Income, Expenditure and Output of the United Kingdom 1855–1965*, Cambridge, 1972.

Field, F. (ed.), *The Conscript Army*, London, 1977.

Flora, P. and Heidenheimer, A. J., *The Development of Welfare States in Europe and America*, New Brunswick, 1981.

Floud, R. and McCloskey, D. (eds), *The Economic History of Britain Since 1700*: vol. II, *1860 to the 1970s*, Cambridge, 1981.

Fraser, D. (ed.), *The New Poor Law in the Nineteenth Century*, London, 1976.

Garraty, J., *Unemployment in History*, New York, 1978.

Garside, W. R., *The Measurement of Unemployment: Methods and Sources in Great Britain 1850–1979*, Oxford, 1980.

Glynn, S. and Booth, A., *The Road to Full Employment*, London, 1987.

——, 'Unemployment in the Interwar Period: A Case for Relearning the Lessons of the 1930s?', *Economic History Review*, 2nd series, 36, 1983.

Gordon, D. M., *Segmented Work, Divided Workers*, Cambridge, 1982.

Gowing, M., 'The Organisation of Manpower During the Second World War', *Journal of Contemporary History*, 7, 1972.

Hakim, C., 'The Social Consequences of High Unemployment', *Journal of Social Policy*, 11, 1982.

Hannington, W., *Unemployed Struggles*, London, 1936.

Harris, J., *Unemployment and Politics*, Oxford, 1972.

——, *William Beveridge*, Oxford, 1977.

Hawkins, K., *Unemployment*, 3rd edn, Harmondsworth, 1987.

Hay, J. R., *Origins of the Liberal Welfare Reforms*, London, 1975.

Higgs, E., 'Women, Occupations and Work in the Nineteenth Century Census', *History Workshop Journal*, 23, 1987.

Hill, M. *et al.*, *Men Out of Work*, Cambridge, 1973.

Himmelfarb, G., *The Idea of Poverty*, London, 1984.

HMSO, *Employment Policy*, Cmd 6527, 1944.

——, *Royal Commission on the Distribution of the Industrial Population: Report* (Barlow), Cmd 6153, 1939–40.

——, *Royal Commission on the Poor Laws and Relief of Distress: Report*, Cd 4499, 1909.
    Appendix Vol. VIII: Unemployment, Cd 5066, 1910.
    Appendix Vol. IX: Unemployment, Cd 5068, 1910.
——, *Social Insurance and Allied Services* (Beveridge), Cmd 6044, 1942.
Hobsbawm, E. J., *Labouring Men*, London, 1964.
—— and Rude, G., *Captain Swing*, Harmondsworth, 1973.
Hobson, J. A., *The Problem of the Unemployed*, 1908.
Howson, S., 'Slump and Unemployment', in Floud and McCloskey.
Hutt, A., *The Condition of the Working Class in Britain*, London, 1933.
Jahoda, M., *Employment and Unemployment: A Social Psychological Analysis*, Cambridge, 1982.
John, A. (ed.), *Unequal Opportunities: Women's Employment in England 1800–1918*, London, 1987.
Keynes, J. M., *The General Theory of Employment, Interest and Money*, London, 1936.
Krafchik, M., 'Unemployment and Vagrancy in the 1930s', *Journal of Social Policy*, 12, 1983.
Laczko, F. *et al.*, 'Early Retirement in a Period of High Unemployment', *Journal of Social Policy*, 17, 1988.
Land, H., 'Family Life in Inner Cities', in S. Macgregor and B. Pimlott (eds), *Tackling the Inner Cities*, Oxford, 1990.
Lewis, J., *Women in England, 1900–1950*, London, 1984.
MacMillan, H., *The Middle Way*, Wakefield, 1978 (facs. first edn, London, 1938).
Manpower Services Commission (MSC), *A New Training Initiative*, London, 1981.
——, *The Employment Service in the 1980s*, London 1979.
——, *Towards an Adult Training Strategy*, London, 1983.
—— (Graham Smith *et al.*), *Youth Unemployment and Special Measures: An Annotated Bibliography*, London, 1983.
Martineau, H., 'Cousin Marshall', *Illustrations of Political Economy*, London, 1834.
Mathias, P., *The First Industrial Nation*, 2nd edn, London, 1983.
Middlemass, K., *Politics in Industrial Society*, London, 1979.
Miller, F., 'The Unemployment Policy of the National Government', *Historical Journal*, 9, 1976.
Mommsen, W. (ed.), *The Emergence of the Welfare State in Great Britain and Germany*, London, 1981.
Orwell, G., *The Road to Wigan Pier*, Harmondsworth, 1984.
Perkin, H., *The Origins of Modern English Society*, London, 1969.
Phillips, G. and Whiteside, N., *Casual Labour*, Oxford, 1985.
Pilgrim Trust, *Men without Work*, Cambridge, 1938.
Pollard, S., *The Genesis of Modern Management*, London, 1965.
——, *The Development of the British Economy*, 3rd edn, London, 1983.
Rees, T. L. and Atkinson, P., *Youth Unemployment and State Intervention*, London, 1982.

Roberts, E., *A Woman's Place: An Oral History of Working Class Women*, London, 1984.

Roe, J. (ed.), *Unemployment: Are There Lessons from History?*, Sydney, 1985.

Rose, M., *The Relief of Poverty*, London, 1972.

Runciman, W. G., *Relative Deprivation and Social Justice*, London, 1966.

Samuel, R., 'Comers and Goers', in H. J. Dyos and M. Wolff (eds), *The Victorian City, Images and Realities*, vol. I, London, 1976.

——, 'Workshop of the World', *History Workshop Journal*, 3, 1977.

Showler, B., *The Public Employment Service*, London, 1976.

—— and Sinfield, A. (eds), *The Workless State*, Oxford, 1981.

Sinfield, A., *What Unemployment Means*, Oxford, 1981.

Skidelsky, R., *Politicians and the Slump: The Labour Government of 1929–31*, Harmondsworth, 1970.

—— (ed.), *The End of the Keynesian Era*, London, 1977.

Snell, K., *Annals of the Labouring Poor*, Cambridge, 1985.

Stedman, Jones, G., *Outcast London: A Study in the Relationship between the Classes in Victorian Society*, Oxford, 1971.

Stevenson, J., *British Society, 1914–1945*, Harmondsworth, 1984.

—— and Cook, C., *The Slump: Society and Politics during the Depression*, London, 1977.

Stewart, M., *Keynes and After*, Harmondsworth, 2nd edn, 1972.

Summerfield, P., *Women Workers in the Second World War*, London, 1984.

Thane, P. (ed.), *The Origins of British Social Policy*, London, 1978.

——, 'The Working Class and the Welfare State in Britain, 1880–1914', *Historical Journal*, 27, 1984.

——, 'Women and the Poor Law', *History Workshop Journal*, 6, 1978.

Thompson, E. P., 'The Moral Economy of the English Crowd in the Eighteenth Century', *Past and Present*, 50, 1971.

——, 'Time, Work Discipline and Industrial Capitalism', in M. Flynn and T. Smout (eds), *Essays in Social History*, London, 1972.

Tomlinson, J., *Problems of British Economic Policy, 1870–1945*, London, 1981.

Treble, J., *Urban Poverty in Britain*, London, 1979.

Webster, C., 'Healthy or Hungry Thirties?', *History Workshop Journal*, 13, 1982.

——, 'Health, Welfare and Unemployment during the Depression', *Past and Present*, 109, 1985.

White, M., *Long Term Unemployment and Labour Markets*, (PSI) London, 1983.

—— and McCrae, S., *Young Adults and Long Term Unemployment*, London, 1989.

Whiteside, N., 'Counting the Cost: Sickness and Disability among Working People in an Era of Industrial Recession, *Economic History Review*, 2nd Series, 40, 1987.

——, 'Social Welfare and Industrial Relations, 1918–1939', in C. J. Wrigley (ed.), *A History of British Industrial Relations*: vol. II, *1914–1939*, London, 1987.

——, 'Unemployment and Health in Historical Perspective', *Journal of Social Policy*, 17, 1988.

——, 'Wages and Welfare: Industrial Bargaining and Union Benefits before the First World War', *Society for the Study of Labour History Bulletin*, 51, pt III, 1986.

——, 'Welfare Insurance and Casual Labour: A Study of Administrative Intervention in Industrial Employment, 1906–1926', *Economic History Review*, 2nd series, 32, 1979.

——, 'Welfare Insurance and the Unions during the First World War,' *Historical Journal*, 23, 1980.

Worswick, G. (ed.), *The Concept and Measurement of Involuntary Unemployment*, London, 1976.

Index

age, 7–8, 22, 113, 127
agriculture: 22, 23, 32, 37–8, 40, 43, 112, 113; commercialization in, 24–6; in Germany, 115
alcohol, 14, 44, 94
Amalgamated Society of Engineers (ASE, formerly AUEW), 47, 55
American Civil War, 30
America: 40, 47, 58, 84, 91, 98, 110, 111, 112, 113, 114, 117, 118, 119, 120, 130; New Deal programme in, 112–14
Anomalies Act (1931), 82
anti-poor law movement, 42
apprenticeship: 27–8, 36, 38, 57, 93, 99, 107, 125, 131; see also government training schemes, training
Arch, Joseph, 26
Asquith, Herbert, 61
availability for work, 37, 55, 59, 83, 88

Barlow Report (1940), 107–8
Barnes Commission, 100
benefits, see state benefits
benevolent associations: 45, 46, 59, 61; see also charities
Beveridge, William, 61–2, 64, 66, 67, 68, 70, 79, 88, 95, 96, 100, 108
Beveridge Report (1942), 85
Birmingham, 7, 81
Blanesburgh Committee (1925), 77
Board of Trade, 52, 61, 70
Boer War, 61
Bondfield, Margaret, 101
Booth, Charles, 33, 44, 51, 59–60, 61, 62, 67
Booth, William, 44

Bourne, George, 24
Bristol, 7, 36, 103
British Empire, 58, 118, 131
British Medical Association (BMA), 84
British Union of Fascists, 118
Butler, Richard A., 96
Butler's Act (1944), 95

capitalism: 56, 58, 66, 68; see also economic climate, free market
casual work: 31, 32–3, 44, 53, 59, 60–2, 66, 78, 86, 128; encouraged, 66, 72, 133; and unemployment statistics, 3
Chadwick, Edwin, 38, 39, 40, 74, 124
Chamberlain, Joseph, 61
character flaws and unemployment, 51, 52, 63, 80, 112, 127
charities: 44; and emigration, 47; funding apprenticeships, 36; see also benevolent associations
Charity Organization Society, 44
Chartism, 30, 42, 48
cheap labour: 1; apprenticeship as, 27; and school leavers, 10, 11
child employment: 22, 25, 26, 28, 35, 36, 81; and apprenticeship, 26; and education, 95; and factory work, 29, 36
churches, role of, in education, 94
Churchill, Winston, 53, 63, 96
City and Guilds of London Institute for the Advancement of Technical Education, 94
City Technical Colleges, 96
Civil Works Administration (CWA), 114
coal-mining industry, 5, 21, 22, 28, 69, 78, 82–3, 85, 86, 112

Cobbett, William, 41
Cockburn, Claude, 85
Cohen, Max, 82
collective bargaining: 10–11, 54, 57, 70, 97, 108, 124, 125, 129; *see also* employers, trade unions
community charge, 9–10
Community Programme scheme (CP), 4, 92, 105, 106
competition: 8, 13, 20, 26, 32, 59, 113; ethic of, 65, 88–9, 91, *see also* free market, *laissez faire*; and funded apprenticeships, 36; and population growth, 24
Conservative Party, 1, 8, 61, 65, 66, 68, 71, 91, 104, *see also* Thatcher, Margaret, Thatcherite policy
construction industry, 31–2, 47, 53, 63, 99, 112
convicts, 28, 47
Court of Referees, 82
crime, 10, 14, 16, 55

debt, 15, 46, 47, *see also* income, poverty
Department of Social Security (DSS), 37
disabled, the, 8, 11, 50, 85
disadvantaged groups: 11, 15, 50, 55, 85; and state training, 108
Down and Out in Paris and London (George Orwell), 103
dockers, 32, 33, 60, 78, 128
Dyers' Bleachers' and Finishers' Union, 78

East Anglia, 26, 30, 41, 43
economic climate, impact of, xi, xii, 1–2, 19, 38, 45, 93, 103, 121–2, 129, 130, *see also* free market, inflation
economy: benefitted by unemployment, 13, 17; free market, 40, 56, 58, 122, 131; and government policy, 51, 56, 66, 90, 113, 117, 125; pre-industrial, 22
education: compulsory, 22; free, 55; reform of, 94–5; state role in, 57, 93, 94, 126; technical and vocational, 94, 104; *see also* apprenticeship, training, universities
Education Act (Butler's Act) (1944), 95
Eight Hour League, 54, 55

elderly: 8–9, 40; and pensions, 8, 23, 38, 55, 63; and poverty, 42, 49, 50; *see also* retirement
emigration, 47, *see also* mobility
employers: 6, 7, 8, 9, 11, 16, 27, 63, 75; and exploitation, 26, 36–7, 105, 108; and part-time workers, 66; relations with trade unions, 53, 54, 99, *see also* collective bargaining; role in training, 92, 94
employment, *see* child employment, full employment, job security, labour market, work practices
Employment exchanges, *see under* labour exchanges, job centres
Employment Training scheme (ET), 4, 7, 105, 106, 125
enclosures, 24–5, 37, 41, 110
Engels, Friedrich, 22, 54
engineering, 5, 28, 47, 53, 63, 69, 99, 112, 128
Enterprise Allowance Scheme, 36, *see also* self-employment
evacuation, 85
Exchequer, 44, 77, 79, 87, *see also* Treasury
export industries, decline in, 5, 33, 48, 69, 70, 73, 74, 76, 79, 113, 128

Fabian Society, 56–7, 66, 95
factories, 28–30, 38
family: 12, 14, 23, 24, 25, 46, 81; and apprenticeship, 27; and poverty, 85; state support and, 37, 102, 116
famine, 44, *see also* poverty
Federal Emergency Relief Administration, 114
Federation of British Industry (FBI), 76
First World War: 19, 26, 50, 53, 65, 73, 111, 115, 124, 127; intensified labour during, 69–70; irregular work and, 78–9; and state intervention, 99
France, 94, 110–11, 113, 117, 120
franchise, extension of, 48, 71
free market, 40, 61, 70, 91, 112, 124, 130, *see also* economy, free market, *laissez-faire*
full employment, xi, 2, 10, 17, 70, 116, 117, 123, 133

gender and employment, 11–12, 19, 29, 36, *see also* women

General Agreement on Tariffs and Trade (GATT), 121
Germany: 47, 58, 66, 70, 98, 110–11, 113, 114, 119; and recession, 111, 112, 118, 119, 120; training in, 94, 115–16, 125; Third Reich, 115–16, 132, *see also* Nazi Party
Ghent system, 11, 120
Gladstone, William, 59
government: 1, 3, 8, 9, 15, 61, 88, 122; and educational reform, 94–7; policy, 17, 19, 20, 53–4, 55, 56–60, 61, 62, 64, 65, 110–13, 124–5, 130–1; international, 114–21, interwar, 70, 72, 77, 79, 102, 113; and poor law, 40; and state control, 56–7; *see also* government training schemes, political attitudes, state, state benefits
Government Training Centres (GTCs), 100, 102
government training schemes, 4, 9, 10, 11, 19, 36, 90, 100, 104–5, 125–6, *see also* individual schemes e.g. Community Programme, Youth Training Scheme etc.

Hadow report (1936), 95
health: 14, 16, 23, 61, 103; as criterion for employment, 8–9; and income security, 45, 63, 128–9, 132; and poverty, 50, 84–5
Heath, Edward, 1, 104
Hitler, Adolf, 115, 121, 132
holidays, 28–9, 66
homelessness, *see* vagrancy
Hoover, Herbert, 114
housing: and mobility, 7; home ownership, 107

Ilett, Isaac, 41
immigration, 6, 54
income: 3, 16, 23, 24, 44, 45, 132; and earnings, 25, 119, 123; and mobility, 48
income support, 16, 71, 87, *see also* state benefits
Independent Labour Party (ILP), 54, 57
industrial revolution, xii, 24, 45, 133
Industrial Training Boards (ITBs), 104
industrialization, 22, 28, 98, 110, 118–19
industry: 13, 70, 75, 88, 91, 97, 98, 109, 122, 123, 130; and state intervention, 99–100, 108, 114; *see also* individual industries e.g. coal-mining, textiles etc., industrialization, trade
inflation, xi, 14, 19, 38, 40, 70, 75
inner cities: 14, 85; and poverty, 44, 48, 51, 58; *see also* urban areas
Instruction Centres, *see* Transfer Instruction Centres (TICs)
Interrupted Apprenticeship Scheme, 100
insurance schemes: 46, 53, 55, 62, 63, 72–4, 77, 81, 87, 88; and trade unions, 52, 75–6, 111, 119, 120, 123, 126, *see also* state benefits
International Monetary Fund (IMF), 121
Ireland, 5, 6
iron industry, 5
ironfounders' union, 29–30
Italy, and impact of Slump, 11, 112, 117–19

Jarrow march (1936), 69
job centres, 104
job security: 11, 38, 68, 133; and trade unions, 46, 52
Job Training scheme, 105, 106, *see also* Employment Training
journeymen, 27, 45
Juvenile (Choice of Employment) Act (1911), 97
Juvenile Instruction Centres (JICs), 4, 101
Juvenile Unemployment Centres (JUCs), 101

Keynes, J. M., 17, 114, 117

labour camps, 113–14, 115
labour exchanges, 56, 79, 97, 104
Labour Gazette, 79, 110
labour market: 55, 64, 66–8, 86, 123, 124–5, 127, 129, 131; and characteristics of unemployed, 51; distinctions blurred in, 30–1, 133; and minority groups, 43; rationalization and reform, 56–8, 59, 70, 127; restructuring of, 86–7, 105, 125; in Germany, 116

Labour Party: 1, 17, 45, 57, 60, 61, 71, 104, 108, 118; and local authorities, 76–7; and trade unions, 80; *see also* socialist ideology
Labour Representation Committee, 57
labour shortage, 6, 8, 24, 85, 116
laissez faire, 54, 56, 58, 66, 98, 109, 118, 121, 122, 123, 130, *see also* competition, free market
Lancashire: 25, 79, 81; textiles in, 30, 82, 83
Liberal Party, 53, 54, 59, 61, 66
Liverpool, 6, 7, 29, 33, 60
Llewellyn Smith, Hubert, 62–3, 70
Lloyd George, David, 74, 99
local authorities: 44, 45; and central government, 71, 127; role in education, 94, 95, 96, 105; in France, 120
Local Government Board, 45
London, 7, 28, 31, 33, 44, 53, 59, 60
Love on the Dole (Walter Greenwood), 81

Malthus, Thomas, 38
Manchester, 35, 43
Manpower Services Commission (MSC), 92, 104–5, 106, 125
manual workers: 6, 22, 47, 52, 64, 96; and casual employment, 32–3; and trade unions, 54
manufacturing industry, 5, 30, 76, 98, 110
marches: 17; hunger (1932, 1934, 1936), 17, 80; Jarrow, 69; *see also* protest
marriage: 11, 12, 14, 27, 29; and benefit claims, 82; Nazi loan scheme, 116; *see also* family; women
Martineau, Harriet, 38
Mayhew, Henry, 23, 28, 31
mechanization: 23, 28; and agriculture, 26; in textile industry, 30
media, growth of, 1, 17
metal industry, 63, 69, 99, 112
middle class, 29, 48
migration, *see* mobility
Milner, Lord Alfred, 58
Ministry of Labour, 79, 83, 102–3
mobility: geographical, 7, 48, 103, 115; incentives for, 9, 47; social, and education, 95

Mond, Sir Alfred, 91
Morant, Robert, 95
Mosley, Oswald, 118
Mussolini, Benito, 117

Napoleonic wars: 25; inflation during, 38
Nassau Senior, 124
National Agricultural Labourers' Union, 26
National Confederation of Employers' Organizations (NCEO), 75, 76, 77, 79, 80
national emergencies, 5, 117
National Employment Commission, 117
National Insurance Act (1911), 63, 72, *see also* state benefits
nationalization, 17, *see also* socialist ideology
National Unemployed Workers' Movement (NUWM), 17, 71, 76
Nazi Party, 113, 115–16, 120
New Deal programme, 112–14
News of the World, 41
No Alternative? Unemployment in British Economic History (Sean Glynn), xii
Nottingham, 25, 29

Oastler, Richard, 41
Orwell, George, 84, 103
outwork, 25, 37, 40

part-time work: 3, 7, 11, 65, 66, 67, 123, 132; effects on benefit claims, 87–8
pensions, 8, 23, 38, 55, 63
Pilgrim Trust, 79, 84
political attitudes, xi, 1, 2, 30, 51, 74, 85, 86–7, 107, *see also* government
'poll tax', 9–10
polytechnics, 94
poor law: 23, 26, 33–8, 76–7; reform of, 39–45, 49, 50, 56, 71, 72, 91, 100, 122
Poor Law Act (1601), 33, 34
Poor Law Commission, 43
Poor Law (Reform) Act (1834), 39
population growth, impact of, 23–4
poverty: 13, 15–16, 18, 21, 22, 23, 26, 34, 58, 60, 83, 84, 131; and casual

work, 31, 67; causes of, 51, 56; and industrialization, 28, 29; and poor law, 33–45; and social classification, 49, 50, 89, 127; *see also* debt, social dependency

printing, 36

Progressive Alliance, 57

protest: 26, 27, 53, 74, 80; abolition of poor law and, 41; and redundancy, 51; *see also* marches, riots

Public assistance committees (PAC), 79, 81

public sector, 2, 4, 6, 66

Pym, Francis, 91

racial minorities, 6, 108

rates: 9; and poor law relief, 34, 36, 37, 38, 40, 42, 43, 76

Rathbone, Eleanor, 33

rationalization, 56–63

'real jobs', 14, 92, 129

recession: 1840s, 29, 30; 1880s, 44, 53; 1930s, *see* Slump, the; 1980s, 5, 7, 8, 13, 86–7

recruitment: 11, 26, 92, 99, 113, 125; influential factors in, 8; foreign, 130

redundancy: 7, 11, 19, 54; and age, 9; and protest, 51; and trade unions, 52, 76

'residuum', notion of, 55, 59, 60, 63, 67, 70, 80, 96, 127, 128, *see also* unemployability

Restart scheme, 7, 9

retirement: absent in Victorian England, 22–3; early, 3, 8, 9, 20; and pensions, 80; state sponsored, 8, 9

Ricardo, David, 38

riots: 7; and abolition of poor law, 41

Road Fund, 72

Road to Wigan Pier (George Orwell), 84

Roosevelt, Franklin D., 112, 114

Rowntree, Seebohm, 44

Royal Commission on the Poor Laws, 38, 62, 96, *see also* Poor Law, reform of

Royal Commission on Unemployment Insurance (1931), 79

Royal Statistical Society, 60

Salvation Army, 44

Samuelson Commission (1884), 126

school leavers, 9, 10, 67, 105, 128

Science and Art Department of the Privy Council, 94

Scotland, 5, 54, 69, 82

Second World War, 1, 8, 10, 12, 20, 69, 85, 98, 114, 118, 120, 123, 125, 133

self-employment, 123, 133, *see also* Enterprise Allowance Scheme

self-reliance, 14, 53, 59, 65, 118, 124

semi-skilled workers, 28, 106

shipbuilding industry, 5, 30, 32, 53, 63, 69, 85, 99, 128

short-time work, 3, 21, 52, 64, 73, 74, 76, 86, 128

Single European Market, 126

skills: paucity of, 37, 90, 103–4, 105, 106, 130; and trade slumps, 7, 52; and training, 90, 91, 93, 101, 108, 126

Slump, the (1930s): 2, 3, 4, 6, 7, 8, 10, 16, 17, 79, 85, 103; European responses to, 111–18; British response to, 118–24

Social Charter (1989), 88

Social Democratic Federation (SDF), 53, 54, 55

social dependency: 11, 14, 16, 18, 19, 50, 65, 86, 107; grants to prevent, 36, 100–1; and state benefits, 128–9

Social Fund, 16, 123–4

socialist ideology, 53, 56–7, *see also* Labour Party

social security, *see* state benefits

Social Security Act (1986), 38

social services, 15, 65

Speenhamland system, 37

Spens report (1926), 95

state: xi, 17; extended role of, 55–6, 57, 58, 62, 113, 118, 119, 124; and training, 99–100, 125

state benefits: 3, 4, 9, 10, 15, 46, 59, 63, 65, 71, 73, 74–5, 77, 79–80, 81, 85–6, 119, 123–4, 128–9; disqualification from, 3, 9, 11, 59, 78, 81, 82–4, 87–8, 102; income support, 16, 71, 87; means-tested, 16, 17, 49, 53, 71, 78, 80, 81, 82, 88, 119, 122, 123, 128; reclassification of, 3, 83–5; sickness, 63, 84–5; unemployment, 3, 46, 63, 71, 73

steel industry, 5

Sweden, 111, 112, 116–17, 120, 121, 124

taxation, 15, 57, 73, 121, *see also* rates
Technical and Vocational Education Initiative (TVEI), 96
technology: xi, 13, 25, 28, 58, 100, 104, 124, 132; and training, 94, 98, 126
temporary work, 3, 32, 61, 65–6, 72, *see also* casual work, short-time work
textile industry: 5, 25, 28, 29, 30–3, 35, 69, 73, 79; casual work, 78; children in, 22, 29; women in, 82–3
Thatcher, Margaret, 1, 5, 65
Thatcherite policy, 14, 41
Times, The, 91
trade: 28–32, 48; pre-industrialized, 26–7; and threat of recession, 41, 46, 75, 118; world, xi, 69, 121; *see also* industry
trade unions: 33, 43, 46, 52, 57, 60, 64, 70, 71, 73, 115, 121, 124; relations with employers, 53, 54, 99, *see also* collective bargaining; subsidizing unemployed, 47, 53, 74; and training, 91, 99
Trade Union Congress (TUC), 54, 57, 75
training: and apprenticeship, 27–8, 36; for black people, 6; in Germany, 94, 115–16, 125; role of state in, 57, 90, 96, 98, 104–5, 107–8, 125–6; and trade unions, 91, 99; *see also* government training schemes
Training Opportunities Programme (TOPs), 105
Transfer Instruction Centres (TICs), 4, 101, 102
transport, public, 31, 132
Treasury, influence of, 70, 72, 73, 74, 75, 100, *see also* Exchequer
Treasury Agreement (1915), 99
Tressell, Robert, 32

underemployment, 21, 24, 29, 32, 47–8, 60, 79, 86, 131
'unemployability', 13, 14, 62, 63, 67, 73, 85, *see also* 'residuum'
unemployment: attitudes towards, xi, 2, 51, 53–4, 55, 64, 121–2; concept of, 12–13, 85–6, 130, 127; definition of, 15, 50, 63, 73, 75, 76–8, 87, 123, legal, 126; identifying, 51, 52, 62, 127, *see also* residuum, unemployability; long-term, 3, 4, 7, 9, 15, 64, 71, 79, 80, 81, 84, 85, 86, 128, and training, 91, 101, 106; mass, 2, 53, 74, 85, 121; and government policy, *see under* government; statistics in, 1, 2–3, 4–5, 12, 15, 52, 64, 79, 87, 128, 129, misleading, 53, in Germany, 116, and recession, 112; as social not economic problem, xi–xii, 13–20, 51, 121–2, 131–2
Unemployment, a Problem of Industry (William Beveridge), 62
Unemployment Assistance Board (UAB), 79, 82, 102
unemployment insurance, *see under* insurance schemes, National Insurance Act 1911, state benefits
universities, 94, 95, 116
urban areas, 6, 28, 131, *see also* inner cities
urbanization, 23, 24, 30, 107

vagrancy, 10, 11, 43, 44, 50, 85, 103, 128
values: social; antagonistic to unemployed, 16–17; collapse of, 10; new norms evolving, 29, 132–3; 'Victorian', 41, 65, 107

'wage overlap', 83, 84
wages, *see* income
Wales, 5, 69, 82, 103
Wall Street Crash, 69, 79, 111
Webb, Beatrice, 39, 56, 57, 61, 62, 96
Webb, Sidney, 39, 56, 57, 62, 95, 96
White, Gifford, 41
Wilson, Harold: 104
women, 22, 26, 31, 43, 65, 78, 79, 86, 103, 108, 114, 116, 128, 131; and factory work, 29; incentives for, 17; and part-time work, 3, 11; unemployment status, 11–12, 82, 88
Woolwich Arsenal, 55
workhouses, 34, 35, 39, 40, 41, 42, 43, 49, 59, *see also* Poor Law
working class: 23, 45–8, 61, 124; and education, 94, 95; and evolving

socialist ideologies, 53; poor relief
for, 49
'workfare', 91, 92, 106
work practices: 21–2, 32, 64, 66, 78,
86, 115, 123, 133; diversification of
hours, 28, 29, 54, 55; reform of, and
trade unions, 46

Yorkshire, 25, 28, 42, 79
youth and unemployment, 7, 8, 9, 10,
11, 36, 97, 100–1, 105, 113, 126, 131,
see also child employment,
government training schemes, school
leavers
Youth Employment Service, 104
Youth Opportunities Programme
(YOP), 101, 105, 106
Youth Training Scheme (YTS), 4, 36,
101, 102, 105, 106, 125